AT HOME ON THE STROLL

"What do you call a man who takes money from a prostitute?
Your Honour."

— from a poster used by the English Collective of Prostitutes

AT HOME ON THE STROLL

My Twenty Years as a
Prostitute in Canada

Alexandra Highcrest

Alfred A. Knopf Canada

To Karen, who always believed in me and this book and who, more than anyone else, made it possible; and to Paddy, Ronnie, Louie and the rest of the flock, whose cheerful squawks, chirps, whistles and trills accompanied me every step of the way.

Published by Alfred A. Knopf Canada
Copyright © 1997 by Alexandra Highcrest

All rights reserved under International and Pan American Copyright Conventions. Published in Canada by Alfred A. Knopf Canada, Toronto, in 1997. Distributed by Random House of Canada Limited, Toronto.

Canadian Cataloguing in Publication Data

Highcrest, Alexandra
    At home on the stroll : my twenty years as a prostitute in Canada

ISBN 0–676–97053–2

I. Highcrest, Alexandra.   2. Prostitution — Canada.
3. Prostitutes — Canada — Biography.   I. Title.

HQ148.H53 1997   306.74'2'092   C96–932135–X

Printed and bound in the United States of America
First Edition

contents

chapter 1

What Do You
Want to Be When
You Grow Up?

I was born a boy, but have been living as a woman since 1989. I spent the first ten years of my life trying to fit into the northern Ontario male mould, and usually felt like I was trying to jam a square peg into a round hole. I was born with the basic male equipment, and my parents tried their best to raise a son, but by the time I reached adolescence I knew something was not working. I looked like a boy, dressed like a boy, sounded like a boy. When I was sixteen I even had straight sex like a boy. But I didn't *feel* like a boy. Had I talked to other teenage males, I would have discovered that I didn't *think* like a boy either. As it was, by the time I left home in 1972, I wasn't sure what I was, but I knew that I would never be much of a man.

I was born in Sudbury in 1953 and grew up in a small mining town located just a few minutes' drive to the north, a town which has since been swallowed up to become part of Sudbury's suburbs. At first it was just another northern town, but in the mid-1960s NASA sent their astronauts to train nearby. The city is built on the Cambrian Shield and the terrain, eroded by natural forces and ravaged by extensive nickel mining and smelting, was said to resemble the lunar surface. Sudbury's image took a slap in the face, but I like to say I spent my childhood on the light side of the moon.

My father worked as a hard-rock miner for International Nickel and retired from the company with a full pension, a bad back and a propensity for migraine headaches. Once I was old enough to go to school, my mother took a job managing the local community centre. She ran the concession booth and made sure that all the events scheduled for the centre went off smoothly. The place ran like a good watch with her as the main spring. My parents took their work very seriously; neither ever took unnecessary sick days or thought about taking a year off to collect pogey. Work was central to their lives and my father, in particular, felt a person's job went a long way towards defining who the person was. In his eyes, lawyers and doctors were better than miners and other labourers, and the last thing he wanted to see his children doing was hard labour, as he had done all his working life.

I was the younger of two children. My sister, Tanya, nine years older, helped Mom raise me. Because of our age difference we didn't really connect as sisters until I reached my late teens.

I recall the Sudbury of the late fifties and early sixties as a pretty good place to do kid things. There was plenty of bush nearby to play in, we could swim in the ponds and lakes and nobody worried about our current urban spectres — drugs, crime and violence. We came when our parents called and usually did what we were told. A bad kid was someone who broke windows on purpose or stole too many comic books from the local variety store.

When I was very young the key person in my life was my mother. We did all sorts of things together: went shopping, ate dinners out — she even taught me to play pool. She also taught me to read and write before I ever set foot in a classroom.

I never had that kind of relationship with my father. He was the authority figure in our home, the rule maker and disciplinarian. He was someone to be obeyed and avoided. In our working-class neighbourhood it was common to see a kid get ferociously spanked in public, whipped with a belt, or grounded for weeks at a time. My father never struck me or used any sort of punishment that would give a present-day social worker cause for concern. When I was disciplined, either by lecture or a reasonable grounding, I usually deserved it. Still, he rarely showed me, or anyone, love and affection and he and I just never clicked.

He thought that because I was a boy I should be interested in the same things as other young boys. I wasn't. I didn't like hunting or fishing, wasn't interested in cars, didn't want to play with his tools and I never fooled around with his rifles and shotguns (Dad hunted). When he bought me a baseball glove, I wrote my name on it with an ink marker, just as he told me to do, then put it away in a closet. It's probably still there. I had a couple of interests that are usually attributed to boys — aviation and history — and I spent hours reading about planes or famous battles. My father wondered why I wasn't out playing ball with other kids my age. I wasn't some sort of young hermit, I just gave in to my interests.

I was a latch-key kid long before anyone coined the phrase. When I was ten, Tanya entered university in Sudbury and moved into residence. My father did shift-work, while Mom worked afternoons and evenings. On days when both parents worked late, I took out supper from a local restaurant and either ate with my mother at the community centre or at home alone. I had my own keys to the house and had the freedom to come and go pretty much as I pleased. I loved this arrangement and felt very responsible and grown up.

The older I got, the less I liked my home town, mainly because I found fewer and fewer things to do. Sports were popular with older kids and teenagers, but players had to possess certain skills to excel at scoring goals or hitting home runs. I was hopeless at sports; I didn't learn to ride a bike until I became a teenager and I never learned how to skate. Baseball, football and other team sports were all beyond me. I was the fat kid who did well in school, not the jock. Every guy I knew hunted. The bush was only a fifteen-minute walk from my parents' house and during the fall, if you went out early enough in the morning, you could hear gunfire in the distance as duck hunters tried to bag their limits. Beirut for critters. This disturbed me because I loved birds then, and still do.

Instead of getting physical I went to the movies and I read. My taste in books ran to fantasy, historical fiction, historical non-fiction, thrillers, spy novels — anything that gave me a decent sense of escape. I've always been enchanted with flight and during my teens I spent hours building model airplanes and learning aviation history, while dreaming of learning to fly. By the time I graduated from high school I could give you a detailed account of the pros and cons of every aircraft used in the Battle of Britain, or describe how ring wraiths were created, but I didn't know the difference between a slap shot and a hoop shot.

When I reached my mid-teens, I, like most of my friends, began trying to get served in the local bars. All of us made a big deal about drinking in bars, but house and bush parties were more important aspects of our social lives. Getting served in a beer or liquor store while underaged was another rite of passage and, thanks to my height and body shape — round, like a big potato — the government sold booze to me when I was sixteen. The house parties, where the ill-gotten booze was consumed, were cliquey affairs. Golden boys got drunk with golden girls in nice middle-class homes while the less-esteemed members of the student body — non-jocks, hippies, troublemakers, unpopular girls — partied elsewhere. There was little crossing over between the two groups. I fell in with the less-popular crowd, so I sometimes went to their parties, but I didn't really feel like I was a part of this group either.

The Sudbury of the late sixties and early seventies was an intolerant city and deviants weren't made to feel welcome. Gay men and lesbians were invisible. Hippies who hung out on the downtown streets were regularly rousted by the police. Native Canadians were written off as drunken bums. There was no multicultural flavour and visible minorities, particularly blacks, stood out in a crowd just because it was unusual to see a non-white face anywhere except in a restaurant.

There was no definable Chinatown but every neighbourhood had at least one Asian-run eatery offering "Chinese
and Canadian cuisine." I don't know if Sudbury was any
more or less racist than any other comparable city of the
time but, being born blonde and fair-skinned, I'm hardly an
appropriate judge. European minorities were everywhere and
the city had its little pockets of Italians, Finns, Croatians and
other groups living amongst the Anglo and Francophone
majorities.

Sudbury was a labour town and a bastion for left-leaning
politicians. The NDP ruled while I lived there and when an
NDP encumbent faced a serious challenger the up-and-comer
was usually a Liberal. Most Sudburians I knew felt the Pro-
gressive Conservatives only represented the interests of big
business and money and the only Sudburian I knew who
voted Tory was, oddly enough, my father. My mother voted
Liberal, having been swept off her feet by Trudeau-mania,
and I always voted New Democrat, so you could say that
while the three of us were together we always cancelled out
each other's votes. Neither of my parents ever got politically
active and I didn't get involved in the morass of politics until
my thirties.

The older I got, the more strained my relationship with
my parents became. Dad and I drifted further apart. When I
was in elementary school I feared and respected my father
and would not openly challenge him. That changed when I
reached my middle teens and we had many loud, emotional
arguments. I was a good student in elementary school but
my marks in math and the sciences plummeted in high
school. Dad began comparing my academic performance to
Tanya's; she had racked up a series of scholarships before

moving on to university. His argument, "If she can do it, why can't you?" made me feel like a failure. My school successes in subjects such as history and English, which I aced, were never acknowledged or treated as important. Rather than knuckle down and hit the texts, I rebelled and withdrew. My rebellion took the form of staying away from home as much as I could, regardless of what my father said. When I was home, I kept to my room and dove into books and model building. During my last couple of years in Sudbury, some days I saw my father only at mealtime, and I thought even that was too often.

My relationship with my mother changed as well. The fights between Dad and me hurt her and she often tried to intervene as a peacemaker, but I thought she always sided with my father and I felt betrayed. Mom also seemed unwilling to accept the fact that I was growing up. I know this sounds contradictory: when I was a child I had a great amount of personal freedom and was encouraged to be independent but as I approached young adulthood I was babied by my overly protective mother. Every time I left the house she would call out, "Be careful," or "Be sure to come home soon." She questioned my appearance, style of dress, choice of friends and what I did when I was away from the house. I sensed she didn't think I could look after myself while doing something as ordinary as spending time with friends in my own neighbourhood. This over-protectiveness drove me crazy and that, in turn, tore me up because I still loved my mother very much. I readily accepted being angry at my father, but I hated being upset with Mom.

As I approached adulthood, my parents made it clear that they wanted me to follow in a newly time-honoured path. I was expected to graduate from high school, attend university in Sudbury and get a degree, land a good job, marry, raise a family, be just like everybody else, and never live more than twenty miles from the parental nest. Eventually I could die, but only after instilling the same pattern in my children. I screwed up immediately after graduating from high school. I had no intention of sticking around Sudbury and I didn't share the career aspirations that my parents had for me. They wanted me to become a white-collared, brief-case-carrying professional. In the spring of 1972 I didn't know what I wanted to do with my life, but I did know that I couldn't spend it in a suit, commuting to an office.

During Grade 13 I applied to three southern Ontario universities and was accepted by all of them. The University of Toronto was my first choice, but I would've gone anywhere to get out of Sudbury. The university attracted me because of its reputation and because it was located in Toronto, a place I had often visited as a child and where I now wanted to live. When I explained my plans to my parents, they were hurt and angry, and tried to make me feel that I had betrayed them by not sticking closer to home.

Of course my parents knew that Tanya and I would eventually leave home to make our own lives. While they often encouraged us to be independent, they would have preferred to see Tanya marry some high-school sweetheart right after graduation then settle down and raise a family, but, since she didn't do that, her going to school and pursuing a career was the next best thing. They were worried when Tanya moved out of the house, even though her campus was less than an hour's drive from home and in the same area code. My decision to leave the area altogether caused a real ruckus. My parents convinced themselves that I wouldn't be able to cope on my own and would likely end up in trouble. Their worrying reached new levels of intensity as their efforts to keep me close to the nest made me more determined to get away. Secretly I feared that if I compromised and stuck around for a year or so I would never make the break.

In August 1972 I moved to Toronto, set up housekeeping in a downtown "student apartment" (a euphemism for a room) and registered for my first year at the University of Toronto. Called The Factory by its students because of its size, U. of T. is made up of many satellite campuses and affiliated colleges. I chose to attend classes at Scarborough College, one of the satellites. This meant commuting on public transit for about an hour or so each day, but I thought I could use the time to stay on top of my reading. Scarborough was offering the courses I was interested in: modern history, a little political science, an English course or two for good measure — and my sister had recently become a member of the faculty. After obtaining her B.A. in Sudbury, Tanya married and she and her new husband moved to Toronto, where Tanya continued her studies at U. of T. She landed a job as an associate professor with Scarborough College's English department. I felt it couldn't hurt to have a friend in a higher place. Thus began my adventures in Scarberia.

I had an unusual relationship with my fellow students. Most of them were suburban born and bred and they considered me the freak from downtown. I thought most of them were nerds. I found the downtown social life of loud bars, smoky pool halls and colourful people far more attractive.

That's not to say I was anti-social while on campus. I enjoyed partying as much as the next person and I wasn't fussy about who I partied with. Scarborough College had an assortment of students who threw house parties on a regular basis and the best of these were thrown by an older student named Don.

Don was in his thirties, maybe even his early forties — in my eyes definitely a mature student. He owned his own business and didn't appear to have a care in the world. He was friendly and outgoing and we got along well enough for me to become one of the regulars at the parties in his apartment near Scarborough College. Regulars didn't need money; Don provided everything including food, booze and drugs which I bought for him from the downtown dealers I knew. I was never asked to buy anything too heavy, just the standards of the time — marijuana and hash.

On one particular November night, we had been drinking and smoking drugs all evening and when I left at three o'clock in the morning I was very stoned. It was a bitterly cold night; I felt like I was standing on a street back in Sudbury. There was very little traffic and I had no idea how often buses ran through the neighbourhood — if they did at all this early in the morning. My room downtown was too far to walk to. I considered going back to Don's to call a cab, but thought it might take a cab forever just to get there, so I decided to hitch-hike.

I stood at an intersection controlled by a traffic light. The street was wide and well lit; no cars passed by. The neighbourhood was so quiet and the air so dense with cold that I could hear the traffic signal clunk as the lights changed. Red, clunk green, clunk yellow, clunk red…. I was getting colder. As I began to resign myself to spending the rest of the night walking out of Scarborough, a small, dark car, Japanese I think, drove past me, slowed, then stopped.

The driver of the car seemed as anxious to pick me up as I was to catch a ride. As I jogged towards the car it backed up the street to meet me. I jumped in, then began rubbing my hands together to warm them.

"You going downtown?" I asked the driver. He didn't look like a freak or a weirdo, just some regular guy going home.

"Yes," he said, "down around Yonge and Bloor."

"Perfect," I said. "I don't live far from there."

We drove off. I watched the driver out of the corner of my eye. I hadn't done much hitching in Toronto but I had heard all kinds of horror stories about hitchers getting attacked by nuts who offered them rides. This guy seemed pretty focused on driving his car. I relaxed and soon the effects of the drugs and the beer began to kick in. Under different circumstances I could have fallen asleep.

The first time we stopped at an intersection, he put his right hand on my left knee and squeezed. I was shocked and unprepared. The first thing that popped into my mind was, this guy doesn't look gay. I must have jumped to that conclusion because he wasn't wearing make-up, or a pink shirt, or anything else associated with the stereotypes. He asked me if his hand on my knee bothered me. I decided to play cool and told him it didn't. I thought if he grabs my crotch I'll go berserk then get the hell out of his car. He didn't, and I didn't. We drove on.

He broke the silence. "You're very good looking, you know." He had a soft, sensitive-guy sort of voice.

I laughed nervously and said something about how I was glad somebody thought so.

"I'll take my hand away if it bothers you," he said.

I told him it didn't, but I hoped he could read the tone of my voice well enough to realize that I did not want him to go any further.

As we drove we chatted about how I came to be hitching home from Scarborough at three in the morning. I found it easy to talk with him and soon felt confident that if I wanted out of the car, he would stop and let me go. It was too cold a night for me to want to check this out though, so I decided to ride this trip out to the end.

Before long we were cruising along the Danforth, through the area of Toronto known as Greektown. As my confidence began to build, I pointed out bars and stores that I liked, as well as my favourite Greek restaurants. As we travelled west, I made some flippant comment about people committing suicide by jumping off the Bloor Viaduct onto the Don Valley Parkway. "What do you think kills them first, the fall or being hit by cars?" I asked him. He guessed the fall. I wanted this guy to know that we were now on my turf. I hadn't told him exactly where I lived but he knew we were getting close. "Look," he said, "we're almost at my building. Why don't you come up to my apartment for a drink, a nightcap before you head home? You don't have to stay long and you'll have a chance to warm up."

What the hell, I thought. What could happen? "All right," I said, "one."

My driver seemed pleased. He sped up and whipped his car through the last few streets that led to his condominium tower. We parked in the building's underground garage and

I got a first really good look at my soon-to-be host when we got out of the car. He was a good two or three inches shorter than me — I'm six feet tall. He had light skin topped with jet black, wavy hair. I guessed he was in his early forties. In the light of the parking garage I could see that he was somewhat nervous.

We rode the elevator up to his apartment in silence. Once in, he took my coat and told me to make myself at home. I collapsed onto a light-coloured couch in his small, predominantly white living room. What I could see of the apartment was white or pastel coloured and looked neat as a pin. Quite the contrast to my storm-ravaged room.

We small-talked for a few minutes until he finally offered me a drink. I accepted a rye-and-something and asked him not to mix it too strong. I still had to get home and I was fading fast. We sat around sipping our drinks and he kept up the chatter. My host seemed very interested in my life as a starving student. There was a tension in the air, the kind you feel in a singles bar or at a house party where everyone is on the make. The man kept up a sort of mindless banter until he built up his nerve to ask me what he really wanted to ask. He wanted me to perform oral sex on him.

I was not surprised by his request. At the same time, I felt I was in no danger, and I didn't think he would try to force the issue. This wasn't going to be a rape scene.

"No way," I told him. "I don't like men — I'm into women ... you know, like, I'm straight."

He tried to convince me. He talked about the beauty and excitement of exploring new sexual experiences and new relationships. I tried to tell him not to waste his time; I wasn't interested.

Finally, after more pleading, I agreed to masturbate him. I could have just said no and left; I'm sure my host would not have lifted a finger to stop me. Perhaps I just wanted to play this scene out to the end.

After he was satisfied, I washed up and made ready to leave.

"You're not leaving now, it's the middle of the night," my host protested.

"Yes, I'm out of here," I said matter-of-factly. "I want to get some sleep tonight." I opened the closet door and began rooting around for my jacket.

"Look, I promised to drive you home, and I will, but I'm too tired to drive you anywhere right now. Why don't you spend the night here, with me, and I'll drive you home in the morning."

I tried to say something.

"Nothing will happen. I'm done for the night. But I hate sleeping alone — I just want a warm body next to me."

I was tired and agreed. I crashed into his large, white bed which was stuffed into a small, pastel blue room. When I woke up, the room was filled with sunlight. I groaned as I rolled over onto my back. I was alone. I listened intently — everything was quiet. I slowly sat up and looked around as I began to recall what had happened. I've had sex with a man! I had a moment of panic. Who knew? What would happen to me? My heart began to pound. Finally I pulled myself together and decided to get out of the apartment. I could sort this out in my mind at home, where I felt secure. I did not feel secure in this stranger's bedroom.

There was a note pinned to the pillow. I snatched it up and read:

Dear Alex,

I hope you slept well. I've gone to work. Last night I promised I would drive you home. I'm sorry I'm not able to do that. I've left you cab fare. Keep the change.

I had a really good time last night and I'd like to see you again. Call me and we'll talk about it.

David

So that's what his name was. His phone number was written below it. A fifty-dollar bill was folded into the note; I shoved the money into a pocket wondering what I would do with it and went home to my own apartment, a mere ten-minute walk away.

Later that day my mind kept wandering back to David and what we had done — what *I* had done. I had no feelings for the man. I didn't even know his last name, nor did I care to. I didn't believe I was gay, yet I had had sex with a man. And why did I know, even then, that I was going to call him back? Curiosity? A desire to see David in the light of day? The money? Well, there was the money, but David's note didn't say anything about any more money; all he said was that I could keep the change.

It was a combination of two things. I found the idea of pursuing this thing — whatever this thing was — really exciting. I wasn't a virgin, but I had never been in any kind of a long-term sexual relationship with anyone before. My few previous encounters were all one-night stands. I had no idea what was going to happen next. I realized he could toss me aside quicker than yesterday's news, but I didn't believe he would do that. Maybe David wanted to begin something serious. If so, how would I react?

The second hook was the fact that David found me sexually attractive. Me — a kid who had been overweight all his life and had never felt desired by anyone. The feeling of being desirable was easy for me to get used to, and once I believed someone else desired me, my opinion of myself changed dramatically. My reflection in mirrors became easier to accept. Trappings, such as hair and clothes, took on a whole new importance. Once one total stranger found me attractive, it became easier for me to believe others would too. The more desirable I felt, the more desirable I wanted to feel and I would do almost anything to gain this fake approval.

I say fake because it is. Desirability rarely has anything to do with genuine acceptance or approval — ask any prostitute. It's not unusual for customers to condemn the very prostitutes they see, while shelling out money to buy opportunities to do the seeing. Sexuality, morality and hypocrisy walk arm in arm.

There was yet another reason lingering around in the foggiest recesses of my nineteen-year-old head. David treated me well during our first night together. He was polite, courteous and gentle, and even though he didn't make good on his promise to drive me home he did try to make amends. This all felt very right to me, but I hadn't experienced this kind of treatment from a man before. My male friends always treated each other, and me, much gruffer. If a Sudbury boy did otherwise, he flirted with social suicide, because he risked being branded homosexual. Homophobia reigned supreme and a peer-identified gay kid could suffer just about anything, from taunts and teases to having the crap beat out of him. In the Sudbury of the 1970s homophobia was tolerated, even encouraged. Real men weren't queer and no one wanted anything to do with a man who wasn't real.

I didn't understand it, but I knew the way David treated me felt right. I waited two days before calling; I didn't want him to think I was too eager. When he asked why I had called, I essentially told him the truth, that I was curious. We arranged a time and a place and we met for supper in a lovely restaurant. He peppered me with questions about my background, school and my goals for the future. Wine flowed like water throughout dinner and by the end of the second bottle I was laughing and speaking a little too loudly. I was having a good time. I didn't want the fun to end and when David invited me back to his apartment I instantly agreed to join him.

At the apartment we had another drink, but there was more on David's mind than just having a nightcap with a new-found friend. I may have been drunk, but my mind was much clearer than it had been on the night of our first meeting. I wondered how David would broach that most delicate of subjects. He got straight to the point — he wanted oral sex.

I wasn't ready for this. I didn't want to agree, but I also didn't want to disappoint him. He had shown me a good time and I felt I owed him something. But finally I told him I was sorry that I just couldn't do what he asked. As I prepared to leave, David helped me with my coat. "At least let me kiss you goodnight."

I looked him in the eye and he kissed me hard on the mouth, jamming his tongue between my teeth. I didn't fight.

"Think about it," he said. "It will be so easy."

I caved in. "Let's get this over with," I said. He kissed me again, then led me into the bedroom.

He guided me through the process, gently encouraging me. When it was over, I got up, ran into the bathroom, and began looking for mouthwash. As I gargled with something green and minty David came to the doorway, looking dishevelled and so pathetic that I burst out laughing and sprayed him with mouthwash. Moments later both of us were howling.

For the remainder of the evening, we sat around and talked, among other things, about the financial hardships of being a student. Eventually David told me he was tired and that he had to go to work in the morning. As he saw me to the door, he gave me a peck on the cheek, then pressed some money into my hand. "This will help make ends meet," he said with a smile. I took the money without question, even though it felt odd doing so. I was too poor to worry about pride, or the morality of accepting gifts for sex. More such evenings followed.

I was concerned about what David meant in terms of my sexual orientation. I told my sister about him, but I didn't feel comfortable telling her the entire story so I described only my first night with him and didn't mention the money. She and her husband regarded what I had done as merely an experiment, an exploration. It didn't matter to them if I was gay, but it mattered a lot to me. I didn't feel comfortable thinking of myself as a *man*; trying to work through male homosexuality would have been one more complication — one I didn't want.

Although I felt no physical attraction to David, I did enjoy our evenings together more and more. I had something he wanted, and I was willing to dole it out in dribs and drabs. It wasn't long before I believed I had some power over him — sexual power — and the feelings were captivating, exhilarating and totally addictive. When David wanted to see me, I never refused. When I wanted us to try a new restaurant or see a movie, *he* never refused. Our quasi-professional relationship allowed me to establish the size and shape of the sexual envelope but David had unofficial permission to try and push it.

For the next couple of months I saw David once or twice a week. The money he gave me enabled me to pay my living expenses and have a little left over for purely fun things. Drugs were the most accessible fun things at my disposal and I spent most weekends in an altered state. School was easy and posed no real intellectual challenge whatsoever. The fall and winter of 1972 were good times.

Early in 1973 my relationship with David changed. He told me he knew men like himself who would like to spend time with me, respectable people who would treat me well. He made it clear that these men could be very generous and asked my permission to give them my name and number. Since our relationship was not an emotional one — I would not even have described us as good friends — I agreed without hesitation.

My "dates" with these new men were very similar to my nights out with David. We would have dinner and then I'd be driven to homes, apartments or hotel rooms all over the city for the inevitable nightcaps. We would share a drink or two and then have some pretty basic, mechanical sex, during which I was always the giver and never the receiver. I was always paid: sometimes $100, often more.

None of the men were notable in any way, but some were friendlier, some more generous. Most of them wanted fellatio, while the shy ones were content to have me masturbate them. I was rarely asked to submit to anal sex, and when I was, I always refused. No one tried to push the issue once they heard my initial refusal — I was friendly, but firm.

It took about four months for me to realize and come to terms with the fact that I was prostituting myself. When I was with David, it was easy to overlook this obvious truth. I didn't think of him buying sex or companionship. We saw each other because we both had fun, albeit for different reasons. I considered the money he paid me as a form of charity. Student aid. Perhaps naïvely, I didn't want to think that he was giving me a couple of hundred dollars a week just for sex; I wanted to think he was doing it because he liked me, and wanted to see me do well in school. I told myself it would have been impossible for me to concentrate on my studies if I was constantly worrying about paying the rent.

Society uses many words to label people who are paid for sex: "prostitute," "hooker," "pro," "working girl" (or boy), "hustler" — and all of these terms are regularly used by the men and women to describe themselves, with "pro" being the the most common. "Ho" is another familiar term, particularly on the street. Its root, "whore," is used far less because the word still carries strong negative connotations in certain circles. Prostitutes' rights groups have been trying to reclaim "whore" and destigmatize it through regular use so that more prostitutes are now using the word. Expressions such as "streetwalker" and "ladies of the night" are rarely used by prostitutes, although they do crop up in the press, or during meetings when speakers are trying to sound polite.

Once I began seeing David's friends, I could no longer ignore the fact that I had become a whore. On one hand I felt dirty and cheap and wanted to tear up the collection of phone numbers and phony first names. But on the other, I was thrilled by the thought that I had something in common with women who had always fascinated me — hookers. In movies and TV shows they were often portrayed as bright, beautiful and in charge of their lives. Before 1972 I hadn't heard of male prostitutes, male strolls or male escort services. To me a hustler was someone who made a living as a con artist, not by selling sex. I never thought there was anything wrong with prostitution, the business has always made perfect sense to me. I just always thought of prostitutes as female.

I grew up in a town where male prostitution didn't happen (at least not so far as I knew) and was never talked about, but female prostitution was discussed often enough. When my mother was managing the community centre, she would dress to the nines before going into work. Compared to my playmates' mothers, my slim, beautiful mom was glamorous. Sometimes a few of the older neighbourhood kids teased me, saying she looked like a whore, or was one. I didn't understand these insults, so I asked her for an explanation. She described prostitution as a job, not a vice, and her liberal, pragmatic attitude has stayed with me.

I suspect my mother's non-judgmental attitude was passed on to her by her mother, a wild woman even by today's standards. My grandmother emigrated to Canada from Europe before the Second World War. She arrived in northern Ontario with no skills, no prospects and no money, but had no trouble getting along. My grandmother took on cooking and cleaning jobs wherever she could find them and regardless of where she worked she always had a man in tow. As a child I remember looking through her old photograph albums. One photo showed her and a man standing in front of a boarding house in Timmins; in another she was in front of a hotel in Sudbury, with a different man. Other photos displayed different boarding houses, different hotels, different towns and different men. There was always a man in my grandmother's life but I don't think she was ever formally married.

By the fall of 1973, roughly a year after I began working as a (male) prostitute, I had become increasingly uncomfortable about my gender. I had not heard of transsexualism (or transition, which is the term I prefer) and I felt totally alone. To handle this conundrum I began to function on two levels: the public and the personal. The public persona was masculine. It was a mask to protect the private and the personal. The real me was female — young, vulnerable and fragile. I finally acknowledged this persona and began to develop it. It wasn't about secretly wearing women's clothes or taking up flower arrangement but was about coming to terms with feelings and emotions that weren't traditionally associated with being male: feeling free to display sadness instead of the expected anger or sorrow instead of indifference. I realized I wasn't a guy, never was.

This response was not a manifestation of split-personality syndrome; it was a deliberate, calculated way of dealing with a situation which was becoming more and more untenable. And the juggling of my gender duality was further complicated by the double life that I lead as a student/

prostitute. There were so many secrets to keep from so many people.

Compared to other women in transition, it took me a long time to come to terms with the gender question. In their writings, transitional women talk about how they felt like little girls while being raised as little boys. I did feel different in my early years, but I didn't consider myself a girl trapped in a boy's body. It wasn't until I reached my teens that gender really became a central issue for me.

Everything began to change on my first day of high school. My secondary school was geared towards promoting science and technology and the school had some of the best-equipped classrooms in the Sudbury district, as well as many highly qualified teachers. Other programs in the school played second fiddle to the technical programs and students taking the non-tech courses were seen as second best. Female students were encouraged to take the non-tech subjects, as were the boys who couldn't quite make the grade. Me, for instance.

The social dynamics changed as quickly as the academic experience. Kids no longer played together; they hung out with their own gender and dated the other. We popped out of childhood into young adulthood without so much as a new program to explain the rules. Life changed from being careless and fun to being complex and depressing and many kids had a lot of trouble adjusting.

I coped by burying myself in books. During the first two years of high school I concentrated on doing well academically, and my marks reflected this. My social life fell away to nothing. I became just another face in the crowd, a nobody in a school with more than 1,200 students.

I noticed that the girls were more attractive and more mature than the boys and I envied the attention they received from the young men. At fifteen I began fantasizing about having sexual relations with certain female students, but I didn't find these fantasies particularly fulfilling until I imagined myself as a girl. Looking back, I can see that this period marked the early emerging of my lesbian self.

I was sixteen, and in grade eleven, when I started doing things that the more popular kids had been doing for at least a year. I took up smoking cigarettes, I began to drink occasionally, and I began experimenting with drugs. Smoking gave me a connection to the students who used and dealt marijuana, hashish and LSD. Grass and hash never did much for me except make me mellow and sleepy — and a couple of beers could do the same thing. I loved acid and other chemical hallucinogenics and quickly became a frequent user.

This was also the year I began cross-dressing. At first the dressing was mainly for sexual reasons; I was bringing my sexual fantasies to life. I always dressed alone and at home. I'd borrow a few favourite articles of clothing from my mother's closets, wear them around the house for an hour or two, then masturbate while imagining myself as a beautiful, desirable woman. Afterwards I'd return the clothes and take a shower. These forays into the forbidden gave me tremendous pleasure but I was always terrified of getting caught in the act. I was careful and no one ever discovered my solitary pastime.

By the time I reached seventeen my cross-dressing scenarios had changed. The more times I acted out the role of a woman, the less important the sexual aspect became. Simply appearing and acting feminine, much like an oversized Barbie doll, was satisfying in itself. Overtly I was one of the guys, but covertly I was happily exploring the growing feminine side of myself.

My cross-dressing continued off and on until I graduated from secondary school and left home. I never thought I was doing anything wrong, but I was very aware that this sort of activity was not acceptable in my home or in my home town. If anyone had discovered my secret, my life in Sudbury would have become unbearable.

During my last three years in high school I was perceived as one of the guys, but I never participated in any regular guy activities except drug use and weekend partying. I had no interest in sports, guns, cars, or any of the other hot guy hobbies of the day. I didn't even show much interest in making it with any of the local girls. Shortly after my sixteenth birthday I had sex with a girl I barely knew, but had no feelings for the young woman and we never saw each other again except in passing. I made no judgment of my own sexual future based on this dismal first night. I knew things had to get better.

Because of my apparent lack of interest in women a few of my classmates quietly speculated on whether I was gay. Whenever these suspicions surfaced, I squelched the rumours by taking a huge amount of acid without freaking out. My friends believed queers couldn't handle booze or drugs. I was able to handle a really heavy stone, so I had to be straight. I was okay.

I was interested in girls, but more as role models than sex objects. I paid close attention to the women around me because I was enthralled by their speech, mannerisms, relationships with each other — everything. I was very envious of what I saw. I was out of place among men but didn't think I could meld into the world of women, which was where I wanted to be. It seemed an impossible predicament. I realized, and accepted, the possibility that I would likely spend most of my life alone. I could deal with that, since I had already spent most of my teenage years alone.

My parents were the last people to whom I felt I could turn for help, but my relationship with them had nothing to do with either my growing feelings about my true gender or my entry into prostitution. I didn't become a whore as an act of rebellion. Leaving home was my rebellious act and my poor relationship with my parents was the key factor in my departure. What I did after settling down in Toronto was an entirely different matter.

When I began working as a prostitute I never gave much thought as to why; the answer seemed obvious — money. If David's friends had not paid me for my company, I would not have seen them.

The majority of prostitutes I've known also entered the Business for economic reasons — the same reasons most people work at any job. If there had been openings in other fields for work that paid decent, liveable wages, many of these whores might have done other things, but for so many women the jobs were not, and are not, there.

In 1988, the San Francisco-based prostitutes' rights group COYOTE (Call Off Your Old Tired Ethics) stated in *Prostitutes Prevent AIDS: A Manual for Health Educators,* "the vast majority of women and men who work as prostitutes have made a conscious decision to do so, largely for economic reasons." They chose prostitution because they wanted to be prostitutes, or wanted to make the kind of money prostitutes can make. They might have declined options such as minimum-wage jobs, the dole, or even positions with higher status and decent wages.

In his 1985 study *The Prostitute and Her Clients,* Lewis Diana reported that many women left traditional careers to work as prostitutes. "What is clear," he wrote, "is that in the entire sample there is not a single woman who could not but have improved her income as a prostitute." Catherine La Croix, the Director of Seattle's COYOTE chapter, claims to have left a management position in a Fortune 100 company for a more lucrative position as a hooker. LA prostitute Norma Jean Almodovar left the Los Angeles Police Department to become a high-priced call-girl. I stayed in prostitution after earning two post-secondary school degrees.

When we meet people who have taken up menial, low-paying jobs rather than going on the dole, we often congratulate them for their initiative, independence and determination. When we hear about single women prostituting themselves rather than going on the dole, our response so often is, "Oh, they should do something else." Why are McJobs more valuable, more worthy, than prostitution? Both may be dead-end jobs in terms of economic and social status, but at least the whore has an opportunity to make some real money without worrying about being fired because a CEO she has never seen or met decides to downsize the company to increase its profits. We can't ignore the fact that there is still real job security in prostitution. Even age doesn't always drive prostitutes out of the Business, although it will reduce their incomes. The oldest female hooker I ever met was in her seventies, the oldest male whore I know of was turning tricks at age fifty-one. In my experience job stress limits the careers of prostitutes more so than other factors, but as long as women are willing to sell sexual services, there will be plenty of customers looking to buy them. How many people employed in other fields can say the same thing?

Protectionists argue that women become prostitutes because they were abused, either as children or adults. Many studies have stated that large numbers of prostitutes experienced some form of physical or sexual abuse before they became prostitutes, the inference being if these women had not been abused they would not have become whores. I question this rationale. The vast majority of women who have suffered abuse do not become whores, and all prostitutes have not been abused.

Another theory I've heard many times is that women become prostitutes because they want to have the kind of control over their bodies and their sexuality that prostitutes are thought to have: prostitute women are also supposed to revel in the sexual power they hold over their clients during dates. This all sounds good. Successful prostitutes do control what happens during a date and it can be exciting to know a man desires you, but these emotional rushes can be achieved in the free market. If having sex makes someone feel powerful, there is no need to clutter up the arrangement with money.

The power/control theory really falls apart when you explain it to real, live, working prostitutes. Over the years I've talked with hundreds of them and only a small minority ever spoke about the feeling of power they got while turning dates. The few women who did speak of empowerment very quickly began discussing their lack of power when we talked of the police, the legal system, their home lives or their future. They exhibited none of the confidence of powerful people.

One theory which I think has some validity is that prostitution is seen as exciting and glamorous. Valerie Scott, an old friend of mine who has worked as a whore for years, often told me how, as a child, she was attracted to the life of the bordello madame or saloon girl as depicted by Hollywood. "These women, who were all whores, always had the best clothes.... They had plenty of their own money, they always knew what was going on in town, and they had a good time." That was how I saw prostitute women when I was a teenager.

This theory may explain why some women *enter* prostitution but it fails to explain why they stay once the glamour wears off, and the glamour does wear off. After I had been in the Business for a while most of the dates became tedious and repetitive. The first time a client asked me to do something unusual it may have seemed exciting, perhaps a little foreboding, or even downright hilarious, but not the tenth time. Most clients of prostitutes are not particularly imaginative and I eventually found much of the job boring. So once the glitter wears off, what keeps the working girls working? Money. Prostitution can generate a decent, steady income and it's one of only a handful of jobs which pays more to women than to men.

During the winter of 1972–73 I wasn't thinking about any of this. There were a number of men listed in my address book who willingly paid good money to have quiet, discreet sex with me. I needed and wanted the money these men paid me, I enjoyed the attention these men gave me. It was a good arrangement that could last as long as no one outside of our growing little circle found out.

I had come to terms with my extra-curricular business activity and considered it an acceptable way to make money, but I was determined that neither my parents nor my sister would ever find out. I was convinced my parents would disown me in an instant if they knew. The more I learned about prostitution and being a prostitute, the more I realized I had to lead a double life and learn to play many different roles. It's no wonder British whores refer to prostitution as The Game.

chapter 2

The Game — Leading the Double Life

Moonlighting as a prostitute while going to university carried risks. If my conservative classmates had learned how I supported myself, I'm sure they would have jumped to the conclusion that I was gay. They would also have regarded me as a criminal because most Canadians don't understand our prostitution laws and they believe engaging in any kind of prostitution is illegal. Furthermore, prostitution is often described as an immoral activity; therefore anyone who engages in it must be immoral. And weren't all prostitutes working to support a drug addiction? When you combine all of these disreputable qualities you end up with an immoral, drug-addicted homosexual criminal, who works as a prostitute. Such a person would have a hard time keeping friends now, never mind twenty years ago. But the potential loss of campus pals wasn't what troubled me — I never grew very close to anyone I met at school, not even my drinking buddy Don. What I feared most was going through the embarrassment and aggravation of responding to snide remarks and stupid questions. I also knew I had no hope of explaining my feelings about my gender to my classmates — I couldn't even explain them to myself.

The reaction of my downtown friends would have been quite different. Prostitution was common in the core and people who lived there were more familiar and far more comfortable with the work than the suburban schoolboys and girls. Every downtown person of my acquaintance knew at least one whore (excluding myself) personally, and generally considered her — they were usually female — a friend. Most of my downtown friends were blue-collar workers, pool hustlers, rounders (live-by-your-wits, jack-of-all-trades con artists) or small-time criminals. Problems such as poverty, lack of opportunity, marginalization and discrimination were familiar to all. The players knew each other and shared many common problems associated with living close to the street. I think this is why everyone seemed to get along; there were bigger things to worry about.

My closest friend during my first year at U. of T. was the rounder Kenny Macdonald. Kenny was, as they say, "known to the police." He lived by his wits. When I first met him he was in his late twenties and living alone in a small apartment not far from my place. He dressed well, usually had a pocketful of money, and had never worked a job or paid income taxes in his life. And that was just the way he liked it. "I don't know why people bother with jobs," he'd say to me, "when there's so much money just laying around waiting to be picked up."

Kenny did not consider himself a thief; in fact he claimed to hold thieves in disdain. He much preferred having his marks give him their money. Kenny ran con games, passed bad cheques, hustled pool, bootlegged, gambled and, from time to time, sold drugs. He constantly schemed and planned his next big score.

Kenny was a regular in the Cue Billiards, a pool hall located underground, in the southern entrance of the Yonge/Bloor subway station. I often played snooker in the Cue; I enjoyed the game and found it very relaxing. Kenny showed me how to turn a game into a business. He worked the room, hustling students and local business types into ten- or twenty-dollar snooker games. He knew how to pick his marks and won far more money than he lost.

Through Kenny I met John the Hat, a Runyonesque wiseguy; John's former partner Harry Holmes, who gave up dealing drugs and took up truck driving to earn a living; Bobby Baldesio, a high-strung twenty-year-old who dreamed of becoming a world-class snooker player; and John Bumps, a soft-spoken, sedate old black man who was easily the most successful shark in the room. I also met Louis St. Louis, a friendly, harmless looking fifty-something man who had spent more time in jail than out; and Les Laroche, a small-time burglar who always wore a three-piece suit, spent his money like water, and was usually broke.

These men all knew prostitutes (a few male, many more female), and working girls often stopped by the Cue for coffee, conversation and cigarettes before heading off to work. Joe Green, the manager of the Cue, served the working women as well as he served the suits that flocked to the room during lunch hour to get fleeced by the likes of Kenny and John Bumps. On occasion an unknown pool player would say the wrong thing to one of the hookers who used the pool room as a coffee shop. He would usually be forced to take his business, and his attitude, somewhere else.

The men from the Cue had a very pragmatic attitude towards prostitution — they considered it work. The guys didn't make any moral judgments about the women and no one tried to save any of the whores from their jobs. The women were treated with respect, something they would not have received in the Scarborough College campus pub. The women responded in kind and never tried to solicit customers in the pool hall, nor did they service dates in the room's toilet.

There was a gay bar located around the corner from the pool room to which the Cue regulars never paid much attention. The room had a handful of homophobes but they had the sense to keep their views to themselves. Loud or violent outbursts weren't tolerated in the Cue. Even the generally accepted "righteous beatings" — "He cheated me out of a hundred bucks so I had no choice but to kick his head in" — weren't allowed on the premises. Problems had to be settled outside. No one wanted the cops coming around the room for any reason. I found that a lot of street-level tolerance is based on this sort of logic — causing a problem for someone, such as a gay man or a prostitute, can cause greater problems than it's worth.

I was treated as a welcome addition to the Cue's core of customers and enjoyed being a part of this fascinating group of people, but I kept my occupation to myself. I probably could have disclosed my activities as a prostitute to some of the room's regulars but I chose not to. They would not have branded me a criminal or immoral and they knew I wasn't a drug addict. A few of the guys might have assumed I was gay, but that would not have made much difference in my downtown social life. I wasn't aware of it at the time but the whore stigma was getting to me. I began to build walls around myself.

In the early seventies male prostitutes were not as common as they are now. Few people were coming out of their sexual closets and discretion was paramount in the minds of the men I saw. Word-of-mouth advertising enabled my client pool to grow slowly but steadily. Some men were only one-night stands. Other men thought I was exactly what they were looking for and came back to me again and again. I always took good care of my regular customers because they paid my rent. If I disappointed or refused a new customer, I didn't worry too much about it because there was always another one waiting in the wings.

Despite the fact that my customers knew exactly why we were getting together, many of them didn't like to admit they were seeing a prostitute. These men rarely referred to me as a such and they used all kinds of euphemisms to describe what went on during our dates. I wasn't a hooker, I was so-and-so's special friend. Our meetings weren't business transactions, they were, well, dates. We went for dinner, or perhaps a movie, or a couple of drinks. Our conversations were rarely about the business at hand. We'd chat about school, life in downtown Toronto, or whatever happened to be on the front page of the day's newspaper. Men with families or interesting jobs or pastimes — things they were proud of — would talk at length about these aspects of their lives. Men with problems ranted and raved at me, or used me as a sounding board for their potential solutions. At the end of the evening a man would rarely be explicit about what he wanted. He'd usually say something rather vague, such as, "Would you be nice to me now?" or perhaps he'd say, "Now let me make you feel real good." None of these guys were interested in doing anything *for* me sexually but a few were really turned on by doing sexual things *to* me. I always discouraged, and usually refused, these requests. As a working prostitute, I thought it was better to give than to receive.

Euphemisms and the role-playing aside, my customers and I always understood what was really going on. The customers knew they had to pay for services rendered. I've always been a passive and gentle person but I could look intimidating to many of my customers. I was tall and solidly built, and usually less than half the age of any given client. I never had a problem collecting my fee.

In the early days many of my clients acted as though they were making donations to a charity when they handed me my cash. These men were all familiar with the financial hardships that students face and they thought their contributions were helping me get by. This was true, but these men all knew I was seeing other men under the same arrangements. It was easier for them to justify helping a poor student than it was to justify commercial sex. I didn't care one way or the other, but when I realized a client was using the poor-student rationalization I played up to it. I always wore my U. of T. jacket when I saw these customers, and I complained about the high cost of tuition fees, books, etc. They ate these stories up, because I was telling them exactly what they wanted to hear.

Other customers simply got off on the idea of seeing a whore who was a bona fide university student. Not all who claim to be are. These guys felt they were seeing a better class of prostitute, not "some dirty street kid." A few of these clients actually enjoyed having conversations with me about the news, or whatever, but most of them simply liked being serviced by someone with brains. Now these guys may have thought me a better class of whore, but they didn't treat me any better than other customers did. Their dates were the most business-like and many of these men were one-night stands.

Most of my customers didn't care what I did when I wasn't with them. That suited me fine. I wasn't looking for friends and relationships when soliciting customers; I was looking for work. Overly friendly customers can make the job overly complicated. As the friendship develops the man may try to save the pro from the Business with promises of care and support and perhaps even love. If she accepts, she's dependent on one man. If the relationship collapses, she can find herself back in the Biz — with a whole new set of emotional luggage. I never expected anything from my customers other than a modicum of respect, and payment. I looked for friends and personal relationships, and everything that goes along with them, outside of work. Keeping boundaries clear made it was easier for me to maintain control over the date.

Working as a prostitute does one of two things to a person's self-esteem — builds it up or tears it down. At times my self-esteem was badly battered by the Business. I was devastated the first time a man who sounded friendly and pleasant over the phone flatly refused to have anything to do with me when we met. Hearing someone say, "No, you're not what I expected. Get out!" as he closed his door in my face was searing. I blamed myself — I was too big, too ugly, too old, too something. When I cried on another whore's shoulder about it, she sternly told me to get a grip.

"Why should you get messed up because of some man you don't even know?" she said. Not the "poor Alex" response I expected. "Men refuse dates for all kinds of reasons. Hit him up for fifty bucks then go out and get drunk. Forget it. It happens to everybody — it's got nothing to do with you." She was absolutely right. I was always honest and straightforward with my callers and I made sure they knew who they were getting. Refusals had nothing to do with me. Of course, my healthy new attitude softened the blows but didn't eliminate them; I learned to cope, giving more weight to the good than the bad.

Business had really picked up up for me during the first half of 1973. I found myself spending all of my days in classes and most of my nights with clients. While I could use the starving student routine to my benefit when I worked, I certainly couldn't use the working whore story to any advantage in school. Dates cut into study time and time needed to prepare essays and term papers. Occasionally a prof would discuss the quality of my work with me and I was often told I could produce superior material if only I focused my attention on my courses. I'd agree, but nothing changed. Things were bound to get tougher in second year, so I learned to manipulate the course schedule in such a way that I had large amounts of free time, which I split between academics and prostitution. The strategy worked and I maintained a solid B+ average.

After spending the better part of a year in Toronto, and much of that time working as a prostitute, going home was hard to do, but out of respect for my parents' wishes, I spent the summer of 1973 in Sudbury. My regulars knew I would be returning to Toronto and since I was confident money would not be a problem, I didn't try to find a summer job. Instead I spent much of the summer hanging out at my parents' cottage. I loved staying at the cottage alone. I would spend hours reading fantasy and popular fiction, take long walks along old, abandoned logging roads, and watch the day-to-day activities of a family of red-tailed hawks who lived nearby. My parents spent most of the summer worrying about my not finding a summer job and having to return to Toronto with no money. I wanted to tell them everything would work out just fine, but I couldn't convince them of this without telling them far too much, which would have only made things worse. As the summer wore on, I spent more and more time at the cottage; I could always figuratively lose myself in the bush.

The summer passed stressfully, but uneventfully. I found the old neighbourhood, and the people in it, terribly boring. The movers and shakers from my old school had left in search of good jobs or new relationships. The young people who were still around hadn't changed since high-school graduation, while I had. Old friendships couldn't be rekindled. Half the time I wasn't even recognized by the people I graduated with. By the middle of August I began missing the money and the excitement and had to get back to Toronto. I returned south and settled into a new address well before the 1973 fall semester began.

I fell back into my familiar work and social habits as if I had never left. My regulars were happy I was back in town and there were new people to get to know at the Cue. One of them was Iole.

Black-clad, pale-skinned Iole had vampiric good looks and caught the attention of the Cue's reigning studs. But she was only interested in learning how to play snooker and she was drawn to me because I didn't come onto her like she was the last woman in Toronto.

After a few lessons we became friends. On the surface we had a lot in common. Iole was a student, low on money and looking for a cheaper place to live, or a part-time job which paid enough to enable her to get by. Iole's search was not going well. She found lots of part-time work, but nothing which paid a liveable wage. If she took a full-time job, she wouldn't have time for school. She found many different places to live, all priced beyond her budget. Iole described her situation as desperate, and told me she was half-considering becoming a prostitute to avoid dropping out of school.

By the time Iole told me her story I had learned to trust her enough to tell her about my own experiences in prostitution. She became the first person, outside of my circle of tricks, to learn the truth about how I supported myself in Toronto. She saw prostitution as a job and asked me to tell her everything I could about it. I told her what I knew, without realizing where her questions were leading. I finally saw the picture when she asked if I thought any of my clients might be interested in seeing her. Many of my customers were married, or in some sort of stable, long-term heterosexual relationships. A few described themselves as bisexual, fewer still were openly gay. I was a walk on the wild side for them. I felt that many of my customers would gladly see Iole, and I told her so.

Iole had the two basic qualifications required for working as a prostitute: she had a sense of humour and she was willing to have sex with total strangers. She would quickly learn everything else she needed to know. Being beautiful is not a prerequisite but it certainly helps and Iole was blessed with an exotic beauty.

Iole became very excited about the possibilities opening up for her and wanted to start working immediately. She offered to pay me a percentage of her payment from every date I arranged for her but I declined the offer. I wasn't interested in becoming her pimp. I had seen pimps occasionally strut through the pool hall and their presence always left a bad taste in my mouth. Iole's second proposition was more interesting. She wanted us to live together, pool our money and share expenses. Iole wasn't interested in becoming romantically involved, and she made it clear that the arrangement would finish in June of 1974, the end of the school year. Her idea sounded just crazy enough to work, and I agreed to her terms.

We rented a two-bedroom apartment downtown and set up housekeeping, and shop. We preferred seeing clients in their own spaces but, on occasion, we did work our dates at home. This required a bit of prearranging — when one person worked at home the other went out. We never worked a *ménage à trois*. Iole took to the Business like a seasoned pro and, with both of us working while going to school, the money just rolled in. We shared our secret with each other, but no one else.

*   *   *

Once I admitted to myself that I was a prostitute, I thought I should find out if I were breaking any laws, and if so which ones. An afternoon in a library revealed that being a prostitute was legal, but I couldn't solicit customers on the street nor could I see customers in my own home or anyplace else on a regular basis. The courts consider this keeping a brothel, another reason why Iole and I were reluctant to turn tricks in our apartment. Seeing customers in their hotel rooms or homes was fine. I photocopied the appropriate sections of the Criminal Code and kept the copies for years. I liked knowing where I stood legally.

When Iole first considered becoming a prostitute she wasn't concerned about legalities; she had visions of walking the stroll in slutty clothes and fuck-me pumps. Although I had pulled a couple of dates off the street, I had no interest in that style of work and I encouraged Iole to follow my example. I believe outdoor work was, and is, the most dangerous way for a hooker — particularly female — to ply her trade. Hookers on the stroll put themselves on public display to attract customers and that makes them visible and vulnerable to every cop, nut case or whore-basher who walks or drives by. Iole didn't know anyone who worked the street: if she took her business outside, she would be completely alone.

The soliciting law of the 1970s made it difficult for the police to legitimately bust street hookers because a prostitute had to physically impede the flow of traffic before she could be charged. According to the police, street walkers were virtually immune to arrest, since most prostitutes don't approach clients, they wait for business to come to them. But nothing stopped individual police officers from harassing working women. Prostitutes, the homeless, drug users and other ne'er-do-wells were often taken to Cherry Beach, on Toronto's industrial waterfront, by rogue cops and other violent men, and beaten, raped or robbed.

Street hookers make easy victims for stalkers because they work the same area, often the same spot, night after night. If something goes wrong during a date, it's very difficult for the police to track down the assailant unless the woman can provide some information, such as the licence number of his car. Furthermore, when victimized prostitutes report robberies or other attacks to the police, they are often told that violence is part of the job, and if they can't stand the heat they should get out of the kitchen. Since busy street walkers might be carrying hundreds of dollars in cash by the end of their shifts, it's not surprising these women are often ripped off.

I have seen carloads of ordinary citizens, often teenage boys, harass hookers. In addition to verbal abuse, street walkers have to contend with such things as raw eggs thrown from moving cars, sprays of water on cold winter nights or showers of broken glass. These attacks usually go unreported to the police because the women don't believe the cops would make any effort to arrest and charge their attackers.

Over the years I've met prostitutes who, despite these hazards, prefer the street to working indoors. Canada's courts inflict greater penalties on indoor workers — escorts and independent call-girls — than on hookers who work outside. A woman who sees clients in her home can be charged with keeping a common bawdy house and can face stiff fines or long jail terms. On the other hand, the penalties for street soliciting (considered a nuisance crime by our justice system) are comparatively light, but streetwalkers are more likely to get charged than escorts because they attract the attention of irate residents' groups who, in turn, pressure the police to crack down.

A surprising number of street prostitutes have told me that working indoors, in isolation, is the most dangerous way to work. "You don't know who you're going with until it's too late," explained one of the many blonde "Debbies" I knew who worked downtown Toronto. "When I'm out here working, I see my date before I commit myself to anything. If I chat with the guy, I've got about a minute to size him up before I get in his car, or tell him to get lost.

"When you work for an escort service someone else does all the talking for you. If you work indoors on your own you get to talk to the guy over the phone for a few minutes. So what! Everybody bullshits over the phone. So you go to some hotel to meet the guy you talked to an hour ago and by the time you get there he's drunk, high on coke, flat broke, or just some lunatic — and you don't know it until you're in the guy's room. No, I'll take the street anytime."

Every call-girl I have met has complained about the isolation that comes with working indoors. She's tied to her phone, and while that may not sound so bad, time drags while she waits for it to ring. Escorts rarely get an opportunity to meet each other. There's no chance to talk shop and swap stories. The women don't exchange information about bad dates. No one is around to offer help if a woman has a bad experience.

During my career I tried working for two different escort agencies. The only time I ever heard from either agency was when they had lined up work for me. Neither service gave me a phone list of the other pros working for them; they wouldn't even tell me how many other pros were on the payroll. Agency managers didn't want their hookers talking to each other because they were afraid we'd all start comparing notes, or move off and set up our own service. This enforced lack of contact between working women heightened the sense of isolation.

Iole had been around long enough to know she couldn't openly discuss prostitution with anyone other than her dates and other people working in the Business. If she came out to the wrong people — straight people — she would have picked up her very own set of labels. Iole, a pleasant and decent woman, would have been branded a slut, not worthy of any kind of trust or respect. It's likely that even her parents would have rejected her. Iole understood the meaning and the impact of the whore stigma without anyone ever having to explain it to her.

Iole and I worked together from the fall of 1973 to the late spring of 1974. We ended our partnership, as arranged, early in June. At dinner, over glasses of fine wine and plates of over-priced food, Iole talked about what an interesting time we had had, and what she planned to do in the coming years. She had studied hotel and restaurant management in school and, with her newly acquired background in one aspect of the hospitality industry, I was sure she would do well. She was through with prostitution. Iole had grown tired of leading a double life; she was looking forward to a return to normalcy.

Living with Iole had done so much for me. She was the first woman in Toronto I had spent any time with and through her I learned a great deal about myself. I never explained my feelings about my gender to her but I had tried to indicate that I didn't want to be considered the man of the house. She quickly picked up on this and we kept house as equals in every respect. It was tremendously liberating not to be saddled with manly responsibilities, and the further away I moved from the masculine role, the more comfortable I felt. Iole let me wander as far away from my supposed manhood as I wanted to go.

Fresh from my time with Iole, I returned to Sudbury, and my parents' house, in the summer of '74. It was like being dumped into a bucket of ice water. I found a temporary job, primarily to avoid criticism from my father and to give me an excuse to spend plenty of time out of the house. Mom fretted about everything, even my weight. During the two months I spent with them, I put my real self on hold and tried to play the dutiful son. By the time I moved back to Toronto in August I knew I had not satisfied my parents, but I had tried my best. It was impossible for me to be the son they wanted. It took me years to come to terms with this basic truth, and to do something positive about it.

Before I met Iole I had rented another small apartment for myself. After Iole and I moved in together that apartment became redundant but I didn't give it up. I even let my family believe that it was still my home. My landlord must have thought I was the ideal tenant: I always paid the rent on time, in cash; I never complained about anything and never caused any problems. He didn't know I was never there.

I didn't tell my family about Iole because the truth was too difficult to explain and we didn't want to go through the bother of concocting an elaborate lie. The sin of omission was the lesser of two evils. If I had told my parents about Iole and our shared home, they would have asked me how I could afford to take on such a large financial responsibility. I wouldn't have been able to give them a satisfactory answer.

They also would have fretted over my living with a woman. "Is he having sex with her? Oh, what's going to happen now?" When it came to dealing with my parents, discretion was the surest way to maintain a little peace.

When I was in my third year at Scarborough College, I purposely rented two places — an apartment in the downtown core and a bedsitting room in Rosedale, Toronto's most affluent and exclusive neighbourhood. I told everybody the Rosedale address was my home, but, in fact, I lived downtown. The Rosedale address was used for work; I had a trick pad in the most NIMBY area of Toronto.

My customers appreciated being able to see me at my place. Men were often nervous about seeing me in their own homes. They were afraid of being found out by their spouses or lovers and for many the idea of having sex with me in the same beds as they slept with their partners was just too much. We sometimes arranged to meet in no-tell motels but they were too obvious and very low on atmosphere. My bedsit solved these problems and allowed me to see more customers more often. The extra money I earned more than made up the expense of carrying two rents.

The bedsitter was part of a monster Victorian reno, a beautiful huge brownstone building that oozed character. The lady of this manor was an elderly, English woman, very prim and proper. She lived in the big house with a school-aged granddaughter. I loved the old house and I thought the bedsitter, with its cozy furniture and private entrance, would be perfect for me. Because I thought the landlady might be reluctant to rent to a university student (who might turn out to be unreliable or noisy), I told her I was a salesperson of unusual retail items. I explained that I often met with buyers at odd times and places, and I would likely be away for periods of time. I didn't want a nosy landlady sniffing around, wondering what I was up to.

We got along well and she readily accepted me as her first and only tenant. This motherly woman was taken aback when I handed her ten months rent in advance, but she was placated by my explanation. I told her that my schedule was going to be irregular and I didn't want to miss a rent payment. She wrote me out ten receipts in flowing, old-school handwriting and I had a place of business in a quiet neighbourhood where I could bring clients any hour of the day or night.

The trick pad made it possible for me to cater to fetishists, customers I had not done much business with during the previous two years. Most of the tricks I had turned were very straightforward. I met my dates somewhere for a bite to eat or a drink or two, then we'd go somewhere and get down to business. The time spent in the clients' homes was short, while the motel dates lasted longer because we were on neutral turf. The longer the date, the more profitable it was. When the word got out that I had a place to bring people, a few customers asked if I would be willing to do a little role-playing with them. I just laughed at this question and replied that I'd been role-playing all of my adult life. No one understood.

The fetish customer always came prepared and most of the gear they used in their fantasies I had only seen in sex shop windows or advertised in the back pages of porno magazines. Soon I was helping older, often overweight men wiggle into bizarre leather or rubber costumes, over-sized school uniforms of either gender, bras, girdles and tarty dresses. The leather and latex guys usually wanted to do very slavish things for me such as lick and kiss my feet, or tongue various parts of my body. I hated this because I am ticklish all over, but these men were willing to pay good money for their privileges. I gritted my teeth and complied.

The naughty school children wanted to be disciplined for being bad. I had to be careful when I worked these dates because I didn't want the sounds of punishment to reach the ears of my landlady or her granddaughter. A loud, exciting (for the client) lecture session, during which I chastised the bad boy while he sat on a bar stool and masturbated, was out of the question, as were really ferocious spankings. These were good money dates and I always tried to find other ways to satisfy the nasty boys without getting myself kicked out of the house.

Transvestite customers were my favourite of the fetish crowd. These men were aroused by the women's clothing they wore so I had very little to do except provide them a space, create and maintain an atmosphere, and refrain from laughing.

The space was essential. The transvestites could have indulged their fantasies in their own homes but those with steady partners were reluctant to do so. Their unwillingness went beyond the simple fear of getting caught by an intolerant or misunderstanding lover. Many saw their activities as sampling forbidden fruit and the perceived wickedness of what they were doing heightened the sexual turn-on. But even if there was no chance of being discovered, playing dress-up at home was just too bad, and that's when people like me entered the picture.

Creating the atmosphere was as important as providing the space. My transvestite customers, like most of my other fetish clients, expected me to participate in their scenarios. My roles were usually scripted — the enamoured lover or the stranger ready and willing to be seduced. The transvestite went through her routine and I succumbed to her obvious allure.

An important, albeit underlying, component of maintaining the atmosphere was tolerance. I didn't think there was anything wrong or weird about transvestism, but in the mid-seventies I didn't represent the norm. In those years it was acceptable for people to line up across the streets from Toronto's gay bars on Hallowe'en night and gawk at or ridicule the drag queens who flocked to the bars to strut their stuff. Egg and rock throwing were common during those annual spectacles and the Metro Toronto police did little more than prevent rowdy heterosexuals from rioting. I never understood this raw hatred for gays and queens. The young men who taunted or threatened them were often the same young men who filled stadiums and concert halls to see glitter rock stars such as David Bowie, Freddy Mercury and Alice Cooper — all queens with microphones in their hands.

I knew there was nothing wrong with transvestism, and trannie dates were my favourite, but it was tough to keep a straight face while a balding, overweight businessman pranced around my bedsitter wearing nothing more than a push-up bra and a pair of skimpy panties. The all-too-obvious erection only made the scene sillier. Laughing would have been a *faux pas*, however. I was supposed to be a professional — a mistake like that would not only cost me money, it would upset someone I really enjoyed seeing.

*   *   *

In the spring of 1975 I began to have serious concerns about continuing to work as a prostitute. I had not had a violent customer. I had never been harassed by the police. I was earning, at the very least, a few hundred dollars a week; I usually made much more. No one outside of the Business knew what I was doing. But things were going *too* well and I was convinced that sooner or later the bubble was going to burst.

I had gotten into the habit of hanging around downtown coffee shops and chatting with bored street prostitutes. I didn't tell them what I did and I don't know whether they saw me as a social worker, potential date, or simply a neutral party passing time. I didn't care, I enjoyed the conversations. Most of the women had horror stories to tell.

Everybody complained about the police. Cops were either too enthusiastic about arresting the women or too lax in arresting men who assaulted or robbed them. Women who had been convicted of prostitution charges complained about the fines, or the conditions in the local jails if they were unlucky enough to have done time. Judges were rated; the tougher they were, the more they were hated.

Complaints about bad customers were almost as common as complaints about cops. So-and-so never had enough money, the guy in the blue Ford was a rapist, the suit wearing the diamond pinky ring ripped everybody off. I often wondered why these women ever came out to work, especially given the financial ebb and flow of street business. There were plenty of customers out cruising on the weekends but that's when the strolls were lined with hookers. Not everyone made money. Business was slow in the early part of the evening but at least the tricks were sober. Action picked up after bar closing but the guys were all drunk and had spent their money.

There was always something wrong for the street workers: too hot to work or too cold; not enough customers; too many cops (except when you needed one); too many girls. Everybody had something to complain about, but because I worked inside and focused my attentions on a smaller but more predictable collection of customers, I was spared the trials and tribulations of street work.

My cash flow was more reliable too. Street prostitutes charge according to what they've been hired to do. Oral sex (blow job or bj) cost $50, straight sex went for a hundred, while half-and-half — a bj followed by straight sex — cost $125. Kinky sex or specials were negotiated. A busy street pro could make a lot of money quickly if she serviced a lot of men, but not every night was busy.

Like other escorts, my rates were based on time. In the seventies a cheap date paid me $100 an hour, better customers paid $150, and anyone who paid me $200 an hour or more I considered exceptional. Anything that fit the loose description of normal sex was permissible, but once the date ejaculated — no matter how early in the hour — his time was instantly up. There are no refunds in my business. If he wanted to go again, we would renegotiate. Whatever the going rate, there was always plenty of room for negotiating. A two-hundred-dollar call-girl might roll over for a lot less if business was slow and the rent was due. Undercutting was as common in prostitution as in any other business, as were customers who tried to chisel down the price. "Well, last week Suzie only charged me $100 for the same thing." Nobody wants to pay retail.

Because of the way fees are calculated, escorts see fewer clients but make more money than street whores. If I saw three cheap customers in one evening I made $300, but it was tough to make $300 during a shift on the street. On the busiest night of my career I saw four customers between 7:00 p.m. and midnight and made $600.

I could have been busted for keeping a brothel — my trick pad — but the police weren't paying much attention to pros working indoors. If an agency escort came forward and complained about how she was being treated by her service the cops might make a move on the operation, but they were more likely to tell the woman to find another job. Complaints from residents groups were more effective in getting the police to shut down escort services, but in the early seventies there wasn't as much anti-prostitution activity as there is now. Independent escorts were almost immune from police interference as long as they were discreet about their work. I was very discreet and even my live-in landlady had no idea what was going on in her bedsitter.

But I was still convinced that my luck would run out. I had no concrete reason for my paranoia but paranoia doesn't need a reason to exist — it just arrives and settles right in. My imagination conjured up all sorts of scenarios, all of them bad. My biggest fear was getting busted. If I was charged with a prostitution offence, I wouldn't know where to turn. I understood the prostitution laws but knew nothing about finding a good lawyer. I would have been a babe in the legal woods.

I also feared getting a bad date. In spite of my size, I'm not a confrontational person and I had no idea how to fight, or what to do in a fight. If I found myself in a room with a weirdo, I was helpless unless some fight-or-flight instinct that I didn't know about kicked in and took over. I didn't want to find out.

Of course the gender issue resurfaced. By now I was having a hard time seeing customers who wanted me to act masculine. I began refusing these dates because I just couldn't do the macho number any longer. I paid much more attention to my fetish customers, particularly the cross-dressers. I dressed with them and got right into their fantasies. They saw me as a kindred spirit and loved me for it, but I began to worry about what working as a prostitute was doing to me. I never thought I'd spend the rest of my life whoring, but I hadn't thought about what I would do after earning my degree. I majored in contemporary history with a little political science on the side. What could I do with a degree in history — teach? Being a prostitute for three years hardly prepared me for standing in front of a classroom.

I decided to quit prostitution and move back to Sudbury following the end of the school year. I'd chalk the whole thing up as an interesting three years, then put it all behind me. I destroyed my trick book and, like the obsessive-compulsive who showers over and over in order to wash away every vestige of imaginary dirt, I purged myself of everything I had bought with money earned through prostitution. Clothes, jewellery, furniture, books, all the souvenirs from a fantasy world — gone. I was determined to leave the Business and the break had to be clean. I paid off all my debts in cash, then packed my bags and moved north with basically the same things I had brought down in the fall of '72.

I took a year off to decide what I wanted to do with my life. I lived with my parents and took a job as a sales clerk in a Sudbury craft shop. Working in the store was different enough from my old job to feel like fun at first. The business was family owned and the couple I worked for were pleasant and easygoing. Still, before long I found shopkeeping to be dull and repetitive, but unlike prostitution, the wages were dreadfully low.

One of the few things I could do with my degree was get into teachers' college and, initial reservations notwithstanding, I did so in fall of 1976 at Nippissing College in North Bay. I believed teaching could prove as interesting and challenging as prostitution, and give me more personal satisfaction.

A student teacher's progress through college is graded on how well she does academically and on how she does in the field during a series of practice teaching sessions. The real teachers who supervised and graded my sessions complimented me on my ability to motivate and work with young students. It looked as though I had found my niche in the workplace. A James Bay area school board was impressed enough with my abilities to offer me a job upon graduation, but I didn't want to work in the land of the midnight sun. I preferred to take my chances in the warmer but far more competitive southern Ontario market.

During my last practice teaching session I became particularly close to a much older, very experienced art and music teacher. She had been a teacher for more than twenty years, and she was a natural. Her students adored her and her peers held her in high esteem. However, there was a glut of teachers in the work force and her school board was laying teachers off. Everyone thought this woman's position was secure, until she found a pink slip and severance cheque in her school mailbox. In the staffroom she broke down and sobbed. I felt so sad for her, and was appalled that the board would dump such a gifted and devoted teacher. I decided then and there that teaching wasn't for me. I stuck out the year, earning my Bachelor of Education and the papers that said I was qualified to teach kindergarten through to grade ten. I never did.

I had stayed out of prostitution for two years but I often thought about the work. There was no denying I missed the money, and not just the amounts but also how often it arrived. For a hard-working whore everyday can be payday; there was no need to budget around two cheques a month. While I whored I never saved money for anything major; budgeting was something everyone else did. I'd turn a date, then go shopping or out for dinner.

What prostitution *doesn't* offer is the security of retirement plans, medical benefits, and protection against theft or violence. Many prostitutes leave the trade in search of these things and, if they succeed, they don't return. Low-paying jobs with no future don't provide security, but marriage can. (A husband can offer the promise of security, if not the real thing.) In Europe, where prostitution enjoys a much higher degree of tolerance than here, it's not uncommon for prostitutes to marry and leave the Business.

Women who were trained for other jobs before entering prostitution, or women like Iole, who learn other skills while working in the Business, can successfully leave the trade when opportunities come along. Poorly educated or unskilled prostitutes have a more difficult time changing jobs. It's becoming more and more expensive just to survive, never mind live comfortably, and anyone who really wants to help prostitutes find other means of supporting themselves will have to offer realistic, viable alternatives. Programs designed to do this have not yet been implemented in Canada.

After turning my back on the teaching profession I returned to Sudbury and my previous job. Working in the craft store didn't pay nearly as well as prostitution, but I adjusted to a different style of living. A straight job put me on a fixed income. It didn't matter whether I sold $10 worth of beads in a day or $10,000, my day's wage stayed the same. When I was a whore, the harder I worked, the more money I made. That's real incentive.

There have been many rehabilitation programs set up for poor or marginalized women, social categories that often include prostitutes who wish to leave the trade. Rarely have these programs made a difference. In 1984 Toronto city councillor Chris Korwin-Kuczynski offered to give the prostitutes working in his Parkdale ward (a part of Toronto well known for the prevalence of street prostitution) help in finding more conventional work. The women ignored the councillor's offer, knowing the new jobs would not pay a living wage. Why would someone who is earning $200 — even $100 — a night, give it up and do something which pays $6.92 an hour?

Advocates of assistance programs argue that the women should leave the Business because the work is dangerous and demeaning. But in a large city, working in a variety store or driving taxi can be dangerous. Scrubbing toilets in a hotel for minimum wage is demeaning. Flipping hamburgers in a McDonalds while a twenty-year-old screams at you to hurry up is demeaning. We live in a world with very mixed-up values, and money talks. Prostitution is the only profession where women earn more than men and call the shots. We shouldn't expect whores to hang up their heels just to improve their job status.

I began to miss the excitement of meeting a new trick, and the rush of being paid for sex. I also missed the wonderful feeling of gratitude and respect I experienced when I turned a good date. Despite the hazards inherent in prostitution, or maybe because of them, the work can be exciting. I was treated well by my employers in the craft shop, but the respect didn't feel as intense as that which I felt as a prostitute after showing a customer a really good time. Many prostitutes say they experience a high level of respect from their clients; my experience wasn't unique. Conversely, when I listen to women talk about their experiences in the regular workplace, I often hear them speak of the lack of respect and acceptance they get from male co-workers and bosses.

Still, I worked for two years in the Sudbury craft store and was eventually made manager. With the new position came new responsibilities. I often travelled to Toronto to attend trade shows or purchase stock. These trips always meant staying in Toronto for at least a few nights at a time. The days were filled with work, but the nights were all mine.

chapter 3

Tricks
of the Trade

We are living in the age of experts. No matter how unusual or mundane an activity, there will always be someone who claims to be, or is billed as, an expert in the field. In the 1970s the enigmatic designs that appeared in southern English corn fields — crop circles — spawned a rash of explanations as to who (or what) put them there and why. Soon experts in crop circles — cereologists — began speculating on the true nature of these unusual symbols and one popular theory claimed the circles were created by visiting aliens. Then, two British farmers, Doug Bower and Dave Chorley, came forward and admitted to creating the mysterious circles themselves. Once these hoaxers told their story, many others began copying their antics. It seemed the mystery of the crop circles was solved (and explained thoroughly in Carl Sagan's book *The Demon-Haunted World: Science as a Candle in the Dark*) but die-hard crop circle experts refused to stop looking for the "real" solution. They refused to accept Doug and Dave's testimony.

Prostitutes who have spoken up about the Business have experienced this same kind of refusal. Their comments on prostitution, whether made at a public meeting or published in a local newspaper, are less likely to be taken seriously than those made by accepted experts on the trade — police officers, lawyers, social workers and, at times, psychiatrists. While these experts hypothesize about clients, the wisdom of prostitutes — who deal most closely with all kinds of customers — is ignored, downplayed or simply rejected.

Years ago a veteran street prostitute gave me a simple piece of information. "We don't call our customers 'johns,'" she said. "In fact we haven't called them 'johns' for years. We call the guys 'clients,' 'customers' or maybe even 'dates.' Some girls call their guys 'tricks' but fewer and fewer girls use that term." Indeed, none of the whores I knew ever called their customers "johns." People who typically use this term have very little to do with the Business. The media, the police and politicians continue to use "john," and most Canadian newspaper stories dealing with prostitution will employ the word at least once. In Toronto a school — John School — has been set up to teach customers the evils of street prostitution. Not Customer School or Client School — John School. Prostitutes stopped using the word "john" because they felt it was derogatory and they don't think all customers are nasty people. By referring to the men as "clients" or "customers" the prostitutes also reinforce the idea that prostitution is a business. Few other people are ready to do this.

The clients of prostitutes are as misunderstood as the pros themselves, and they often get a worse rap. During the

1980s and early 1990s whenever prostitutes were unjustly blamed for this or that, some organization, usually a women's group or a prostitutes' rights group, would rise to the defence of the blighted whores and try to set the record straight. I did this kind of media damage control for a few years and other women did it long before I got political. Customers have never received this kind of support in Canada, and to my knowledge no client has come forward to speak out in favour of himself and his peers. (I'm ignoring the badly disguised clients who are often trotted out on American television talk shows.) This lack of voice has allowed the media to define for us what a customer is and the popular press has not painted a pretty or an accurate picture. We're told the clients of prostitutes aren't nice people: they treat their whores indifferently at best or violently at worst; they are noisy, dirty, vulgar men who think nothing of coming onto any woman on the street, regardless of her age, appearance, or reason for being out in public. Those who believe all prostitution is a form of oppression complain that customers are not charged by the police as frequently as the prostitutes, as if men were immune to arrest because of their gender. Clients are often depicted as lousy husbands (good husbands don't go out looking for whores) and even lousier fathers (newspapers delight in mentioning baby seats seen in customers' cars). While there certainly are noisy, vulgar customers who are lousy husbands and fathers, they are not representative of all. It has simply become too easy for us to accept the media depictions broadcast into our homes during thirty-second sound bites.

My customers came from every class of society. Some had influence and social status, most did not. Some of my customers were involved in happy relationships and they truly loved their partners. Others were lonely single men seeking companionship spiced with a little physical intimacy. Most of my customers were ordinary looking, some were handsome; I never saw anyone who deserved to be described as ugly. Some men were very generous; others were real cheapskates. I became good friends with a few of my customers, but the majority of the men I saw were only business acquaintances. The "typical" client is essentially the guy next door. Any man can fit the *real* profile of the customer of a prostitute.

Most guys who came to see me didn't look, sound or act as if they would need to pay for sex. At first this seemed odd to me, considering how readily available free sex was in the 1970s and early 1980s. A few drinks, a couple of good lines and — poof! — the bedroom doors opened and odds were the guys didn't even have to wear condoms. But then there is always the morning after. Men are expected to say something more than, "Well, I'll see you...." Since the seventies the casual sex scene has become much more complicated. AIDS tossed a wet blanket over many amorous adventurers, and there was a growing trend which promoted marriage and family values while condemning promiscuity. While casual sex has become harder to get, laws affecting rape and other forms of sexual assault have become more encompassing. All of this may bode well for prostitutes: it's well known among thinking whores that the more sexually regulated a society becomes, the better business gets.

Prostitutes make it easy for men to have anonymous, uncomplicated sex. This basic truth has brought customers to pros for as long as women have been hanging red lanterns in their windows. Customers don't have to tell their whores anything they don't wish to. A customer doesn't feel compelled to tell the pro that he will love and respect her in the morning. He may say these things but everyone concerned knows they're meaningless words. A client doesn't have to explain where he was last night; he doesn't have to remember his whore's birthday. Hearts and flowers are replaced by dollars and sex. This sort of arrangement may seem distasteful to some — not everyone is willing to accept the idea of sex without love — but non-committal sex still happens in the dating scene. In a prostitute-client relationship pick-up lines and cocktails play second fiddle to money.

During my early years in the Business customers came to me because I was convenient and discreet. Closeted gays and the gay-curious spent time with me without fear of having their secrets revealed. Once I started seeing fetishists I realized that I, and perhaps all other prostitutes, offered another commodity that was often valued more than sex or discretion — tolerance. My cross-dressers knew that I didn't think their pastime was funny or perverted. I never laughed at anyone unless I was asked to by a client (the laughing being a part of the paid-for scene). I never criticized or scoffed at anyone because of their sexual bent. If a prospective client asked me to participate in something I thought was too weird or disgusting, I would just refuse and suggest he call someone else. The longer I worked as a whore, the more I realized that tolerance doesn't always go hand in hand with love. Many of my customers were involved in long-term relationships and they often spoke about the love shared with their partners. Unfortunately many of these same men told me stories about how they had to suppress certain facets of themselves when they were with their partners. I'm not talking about anything too far-fetched here; I'm talking about the cross-dresser whose wife wouldn't allow him to dress up at home because she thought the activity was sick, or the old foot fetishist who wasn't allowed to worship his wife's feet because she felt his interest was perverted. The only safe way these men could explore and enjoy their fetishes was with a prostitute. Whether they should have indulged their fantasies, knowing that their partners were repulsed by the activities, is one of those debates that can go on forever. The debate is really about making compromises in a relationship, and when it comes to this sort of negotiation virtually anything goes. I'm convinced that if many of my customers had had more tolerant partners they would never have come to me.

Any prostitute can tell you about clients who pay the going rate but just want to talk, à la *Irma la Douce*. I only had a few of these customers but I always wished I had more. These men hired me just like any other customer but I never had any form of sex with them. Sex wasn't a part of their request, although it was always available. Talkers wanted a patient ear and I'm a good listener. As the hours ticked by, I listened to stories about bad bosses and meaningless jobs, wives who didn't understand their husbands, or kids who were doing really well in school. I was even shown photographs. My talking customers could have gotten themselves some therapy or chatted with their buddies, but for a number of reasons, ranging from a mistrust of therapists to a simple desire to be with a prostitute, they came to me. I always felt these men should have talked to their partners or friends, but whenever I felt comfortable enough with a customer to say so, I was told they "just wouldn't understand." Talkers believed I *could* understand them, or if I didn't, at least I wouldn't fly off the handle. It's called tolerance.

One of the myths about prostitution is that male hookers and their customers are all gay. This isn't true. Many male prostitutes, particularly male street prostitutes, are heterosexual, as are many of their customers, and it's not unusual for a customer to see both male and female pros. One well-to-do customer I had, who openly admitted to seeing pros of both genders, said that as long as he was paying for sex he might as well sample everybody's wares. During the early years of my career all of my customers thought of me as male but very few described themselves as homosexual. The majority said they were either heterosexual or bisexual and, even considering the number of closed closets there were in the seventies, I had no reason to doubt them. I made every effort to create a safe, comfortable atmosphere for my clients, and told them that their personal sexual orientation was of no concern to me.

Heterosexual people often have fantasies about homosexual sex. While it's relatively easy for women to explore this fantasy (few eyebrows are raised when two women dance together, touch each other or live together), it can be tough for men. "What if someone sees me, what if I like it too much, what if I'm gay…?" Their concerns go on and on. Male prostitutes offer one way for gay-curious men to explore homosexual fantasies. In my experience, these dates were often brief, there was little quibbling about the money, and the customers were usually one-night stands. The gay-curious fellows came from everywhere and the one thing — the only thing — they had in common was their curiosity.

Most of the gay men I saw were very focused on youth and body image. When I could present myself as a slim, youthful man they were happy, but as I got older — and bigger — it became more difficult for me to visually please them. I had little trouble satisfying gay fetishists but I gave up trying to entice other, more traditional gay customers who looked for young, hard-bodied, straight-looking whores. Discouraging these customers was easy; all I had to do was give my real age over the phone, then say I looked my age. "Hello … hello?"

Gay men are believed to be more promiscuous than heterosexual men and the gay community is seen to be more open and tolerant of all things sexual than the straight. Whenever I visited a gay singles bar I saw open displays of sexuality as a matter of course and the action was usually much hotter than in the heterosexual equivalent. In a gay pick-up bar everybody seems to be on the make and couples pair up quickly and easily. Although these non-committal one-night stands may be common, there are still customers for male prostitutes. An encounter with a prostitute remains the least fussy form of sex and the most anonymous. The customers don't have to seduce the prostitutes or entice them with words and deeds; all they have to do is whip out their wallets.

As for female clients, there aren't any in Canada. Canadian women don't sit in hotel rooms shopping the escort ads nor do they cruise the strolls looking for hard young male (or sexy female) bodies for hire. Occasionally I've found "Only Women Need Apply" ads placed in entertainment tabloids by male prostitutes but when I've tracked these ads I've found that they're short-lived. Male hookers don't attract enough business — at least not enough female business — to warrant their twenty-dollar-per-week ads. American tabloid television has tried to show us that there is a growing number of wealthy, older, liberated women willing and eager to buy sex from men young enough to be their sons, but, as far as I've been able to determine, these scenarios don't exist in Canada. There may be a few women travelling to developing nations with the idea of buying sex, but men make up the vast majority of customers in the sex-tourism industry.

North American women aren't socially acclimatized to seek out and hire prostitutes. Most have been taught to be the pursued, not the pursuer. A woman can still cause a stir in a room simply by asking a strange man to dance, or buying him a drink; offering to buy his sexual services exists only in fantasies. In North America it's still not cool for men or women to wander too far from their assigned gender roles and the woman's role certainly does not include hiring hookers.

I've often heard men and women say that women don't need to buy sex; they can always get it for free. I don't accept this glib statement. Many of the men I saw for a fee could easily have found sex in the free market. They came to me because I offered more than just availability; I offered convenience, discretion, tolerance — even variety. These features can be appreciated as much by a woman looking for casual sex as a man.

There are a couple of other very simple reasons why women do not hire prostitutes. When a man puts himself into an intimate situation with a pro he has very little to fear. Condoms and safer sex practices can prevent the transmission of sexually transmitted diseases (STDs) and it's highly unlikely the prostitute will try to physically overpower the customer. Most men are stronger than most women so male customers have little need to worry about being assaulted by the whores they hire. If the roles were reversed, I doubt if the female customers would feel as secure. Furthermore, commercial sex is a luxury and, in most cases, an expensive one. Men have more disposable income than women. Even if women could feel safe and comfortable hiring prostitutes, most could not afford to do so. And there is yet another factor which cannot be ignored: most of the sex sold by prostitutes is very mechanical — a fast-food version of physical intimacy. As a woman, I've never wanted this kind of sex in my personal life; I've never met a woman who did. Why buy an unsatisfying service?

Ordinary men who frequent prostitutes rarely attract much individual attention. We never see headlines announcing: "John Q. Citizen arrested for hiring streetwalker." Ordinary men generally act the same as the rich and famous when it comes to keeping the lid on their covert sexual activities. The closet is king. Accordingly, it was rather surprising when fifty-three-year-old Ontario Conservative backbencher Bill Vankoughnet was picked up during a police john sweep in Toronto's Parkdale in May 1996. What was he doing on the stroll when there are far less obvious ways of procuring the services of a prostitute? To the best of my knowledge, no one thought to ask him, at least not in public. Rather than going to trial, Vankoughnet, known as an exponent of family values, opted to sneak out the legal back door and signed up for Toronto's John School. Under this program, men charged with communicating with a prostitute for the first time have the option of going to trial or attending a day-long "school," for which they pay $250, and receiving a conditional discharge with no criminal record. Following his "graduation," the once-exiled MPP was welcomed back into the provincial Tory caucus. (One of my old customers was formerly a member of the Canadian Armed Forces and during his career one of his duties involved acquiring prostitutes for a well-known and highly placed Canadian politician. Vankoughnet could have learned a thing or two from this man.)

Like Vankoughnet, regular guys who get pinched in sweeps look for the quietest way out rather than confront the issue in court, which could mean being noticed by the media and exposed to family and friends. When men do speak openly about hiring hookers, it's usually in bars, after fuelling up on liquid courage. The stories are often set in foreign countries, or took place years ago. "Yeah, when I was in university I spent a summer in Amsterdam, and boy did I …" Nobody wants to be known as a customer — a john — cruising the streets in their home town or flipping through the escort ads in the papers looking for sex *tonight*. Nobody wants the stigma.

Occasionally a celebrity will admit to hiring hookers, usually after getting busted or outed by a pro or madam, and he'll often do it with a "yeah, so what" kind of attitude. The celebs who admit this have usually manufactured a reputation for being rebellious, unpredictable and wild. These spoiled brat rich kids looking to enlarge their public profiles must believe there is no such thing as bad publicity; as long as no serious taboos are crossed, anything goes. Hugh Grant, British actor and suitor to a well-known model, earned more press by getting caught with a Hollywood street hooker than he ever got for appearing in a movie. We are fascinated whenever someone famous is implicated in the commercial sex industry. When Heidi Fleiss, the latest Hollywood madam to be taken down by the police, was busted for running an escort service, the tabloid-tuned world waited with baited breath to discover which Hollywood bigshots hired whores, and what they did with them. The movie moguls became johns in the derogatory sense and we wanted to see them fall from grace. Fleiss kept her mouth and her trick book shut, disappointing talk-show audiences around the world.

Dating prostitutes may not be a big deal in tinsel town, unless of course the pro happens to be the same sex as the customer, but among the general public being a john is taboo — one I've never accepted. It's always been fine for men to actively seek out sex partners. Sexually active boys are heroes in school and school heroes, particularly sports heros, are assumed to be sexually active. Sexually active women are stigmatized in North American society but randy men are at least forgiven, if not celebrated. But when men dispense with the flirting and courting that goes on in singles bars and choose to cut to the chase and hire hookers, they become bad people. It doesn't matter whether the man is single or in a relationship, has a family at home or is looking for his first sexual encounter, if he's a john, he's flawed.

When I moved to Toronto in 1972, Yonge Street, between Bloor and King streets, was the most active stroll in the city. Strip clubs and massage parlors shared Toronto's crass commercial heartland with restaurants, theatres and myriad stores. The Strip had a vibrancy found nowhere else in the city and the neon excitement attracted people from all over the country. The Strip also attracted hookers of every shape and size. Women who weren't working in the massage parlours could be found in front of every strip club; hanging out, smoking cigarettes and waiting for their next tricks. These women chatted with tourists and curiosity seekers as readily as they chatted with serious customers, just in case they could convince the guys from small-town Canada, or the bar next door, to spring for quick tumbles in the nearby trick hotels.

Not everybody wanted the sex trade on Toronto's most famous street but business went on as usual until 1977, when everything changed. Emanuel Jaques, a fourteen-year-old shoeshine boy who some believed also worked as a prostitute, was murdered above a Yonge and Dundas massage parlour. Although Jaques's death had nothing to do with the massage parlour, the tragedy sparked a massive campaign to clean up the Strip. A municipal by-law shut down the parlours and the women working in them were forced outside (thereby increasing the number of streetwalkers) — then driven off Yonge Street altogether.

The prostitutes didn't go far. Before long they were plying their trade on the major secondary streets which parallel Yonge; Church, Jarvis and Sherbourne. These streets were zoned commercial-residential and the prostitutes began rubbing shoulders with Toronto's downtown residents. Customers and curiosity seekers followed the whores when they migrated east and the night-time traffic volume increased on these previously quiet streets. The police could do little to stop the shifting of the trade.

During the campaign to clean up Yonge Street many trick hotels and flop houses were shut down. The availability of trick hotels — places where rooms can be rented cheaply and discreetly — is important to people involved in street prostitution. Not all customers have places to take prostitutes and many streetwalkers dislike leaving their familiar neighbourhoods to turn dates. With the closing of the downtown trick hotels prostitutes and their customers were deprived of nearby places to go to have sex. People began having commercial sex (as well as free sex) in public or semi-secluded private places — lanes and alcoves, backyards or parked cars. The residents living in neighbourhoods frequented by pros and their customers — Cabbagetown in downtown Toronto and South Parkdale in the city's west end — wanted none of this and the clients were eventually targeted as being a big part of the problem.

Grassroots anti-prostitute activism in all North American cities follows a very regular pattern. First the residents groups go after the pros, and when that fails, they put pressure on the customers in an effort to keep the guys out of their neighbourhoods. The rationale is if you eliminate the demand you eliminate the business. Clients are accused of littering, being noisy, and verbally or physically assaulting women. At the same time, the sex trade is blamed for other, unrelated crimes in the area, and for the spread of the drug trade. The customers have little to do with these problems.

I know some customers do litter. The most commonly requested service on the street is the bj — the blow job, oral sex — because it's fast, cheap and can easily be performed in a car. When a man receives a bj in his vehicle, or in an alley or doorway, he's left with the used condom to dispose of. We all know what he does with it — he peels it off and throws it away. Discarded condoms are found in parks, on sidewalks, sometimes even in private yards. Regardless of who put them there (pros and their customers aren't the only people who have sex in unusual places), customers are blamed for the litter.

In Centrum, the red-light district of Amsterdam, prostitution is much more open than on any stroll in Canada. When my partner Karen Maki and I visited the city in 1992 and again in 1993, we stayed in Centrum both times and we saw few discarded condoms. In Amsterdam it's easy for pros and their customers to find places to go to take care of business and during the times we were there we never heard an Amsterdammer complain about the problems caused by customers. In Canadian cities the opposite is true — commercial sex happens in all sorts of inappropriate places and the tell-tale signs are left behind.

Customers will follow street prostitutes all over a city. If the pros are forced out of one neighbourhood, they just move into another. The customers follow, as do the "circle jerks" and gawkers who drive around the strolls watching what goes on, often taunting and teasing anyone on the street. Circle jerks are not out to shop, they are out to raise hell. It's virtually impossible for residents to tell the difference, so they assume that the customers are causing problems. I would think that common sense would tell people that most customers are not out on the street to attract attention to themselves. They know they are committing a criminal offence. Even if they don't think the law is just, they're not about to announce to the world that they are out there breaking it. Street prostitutes have argued that circle jerks are the cause of noise and other nuisances. Occasionally prostitutes are able to get this message across to residents groups by speaking up at community meetings, but nothing gets done and the noise and harassment go on. The police charge thousands of prostitutes and their customers annually but the problems never go away. Could it be the street-walkers are right and the wrong people are being arrested? Innovative solutions to these problems are seldom considered seriously and rarely acted upon. In Toronto the Works Department has never even installed more garbage containers in neighbourhoods where residents have complained about discarded condoms, needles and other street refuse.

Residents' groups try to discourage customers from coming into their neighbourhoods by threatening them with video cameras and other recording devices and, ultimately, exposure. The police go so far as to entrap customers with elaborate sting operations. But regardless of the amount of heat on the street, many men hire street prostitutes because they are less expensive than call-girls. Action on the stroll often costs less than half the cost of action inside.

It is a common belief that customers play a large role in one of the major problems associated with prostitution — violence. It's assumed that customers regularly beat up or rob whores, or do worse. I had my teeth kicked in and was almost stabbed by a berserk client in the Holiday Inn in Sault Ste. Marie, but this was the only time I was injured while working. The vast majority of clients do not look for any kind of trouble at all. Blaming all customers for the violence inflicted on pros makes as much sense as blaming all the people who shop in convenience stores for convenience-store robberies. The criminal actions of a few cannot be regarded as examples of typical behaviour.

While the vast majority of customers are not violent, it is true that violent men will prey on prostitutes, particularly street prostitutes, because they're visible and accessible, and the police don't always heed their complaints. Over the last few years the police have become more responsive to reports of violence filed by pros, but in many ways street prostitutes still appear, in the eyes of a few, as ideal victims.

Serial killers have been murdering pros at least since the nineteenth century. From 1861 to 1864 Parisian serial murderer Joseph Philippe killed three women and attempted to kill three more. Four of his victims, including the first, were prostitutes. Philippe killed for money, robbing his victims after murdering them. The infamous Jack the Ripper sliced up five Whitechapel hookers in 1888. Jack the Stripper (so named because all of his victims were found nude) slew six women, all prostitutes, in London between February 1964 and February 1965. No one knows why either Jack went on his rampage because neither was caught; the police believe both simply died. During his five-year career Peter Sutcliffe, the Yorkshire Ripper, killed thirteen women and tried to kill seven more. Eight of the slain were prostitutes, and we know why Sutcliffe murdered them — he believed he was on a divine mission. "I was just cleaning up the streets," he told his brother after his trial in 1981. Closer to home, Los Angeles' South Side Slayer murdered seventeen black women, all prostitutes, during the mid-1980s. The Los Angeles Police Department waited until ten women were dead before they told the public that a serial killer was on the loose.

Men who rob, assault and sometimes kill prostitutes aren't customers who have gone bad, they're criminals who pose as customers until they bring their victims into striking range. Men who harm pros will attack other women, and violence inflicted on prostitutes is only a part of the larger problem of violence against women. As efforts to eliminate these assaults become more effective, prostitution-related violence will also decrease. Programs such as the John School are nothing more than localized Band-aid solutions. John School participants are lectured by lawyers, cops, public health officials and residents on the legal aspects of prostitution, sexually transmitted diseases and the impact of the Business on neighbourhoods. Former prostitutes talk about life on the street, why they got into the Biz and why they see themselves as victims. The purpose of John School is to stop the "students" from reoffending. It won't stop the blood flowing.

Prostitutes' rights organizations have tried to explain how programs that attempt to drive customers from the strolls actually endanger women. The only men who are likely to be affected by customer-deterrent actions such as police sweeps and John Schools are the kind of men who make good customers. Once the regular-guy customers are scared off, the only ones left are the rowdies and the sort of men who don't mind running the risk of getting arrested. These are the very people likely to cause trouble for the pros and the neighbourhoods they work in. Clearly the anti-john campaigns create a lose-lose situation. The prostitutes lose because they're forced to take more risks over a longer period of time in order to earn less money. Neighbourhoods lose because the men causing the problems are not deterred and the problems don't go away, even though scarce police resources — resources that could be used to combat more threatening crime — are used in john crack-downs.

Opponents of Canada's prostitution laws have described anti-john campaigns as classist and say the laws penalizing customers discriminate against the poor. Section 213 of our Criminal Code, the communicating law, which took effect in 1985, makes it an offence for anyone to communicate in a public place (the street, a park, a bar, even your car is considered a public place under this law) for the purpose of prostitution. Hookers are charged for chatting up their customers and customers are charged for talking with whores. At first far more whores were getting busted then their male customers, but over the last few years police forces have taken steps to even up the numbers. I know the prostitutes aren't pleased with this turn of events and neither are the customers. When it comes to the penalties for being convicted of communicating — a far more important issue — the women lead the pack. Prostitutes who reoffend often end up in jail, but I've never heard of a client doing time for simple communicating.

While the police busy themselves sweeping the streets of clients, men can see escorts and call-girls with virtual impunity. Escorts and freelance call-girls are the most invisible of prostitutes while streetwalkers are the most visible; brothels fall somewhere in between. We have laws which are designed to deter men from hiring street hookers and from visiting brothels but there are no laws preventing anyone from hiring call-girls. This leads me to believe that the real purpose of these laws is to force the Business behind closed doors and keep it there. They're not designed to eliminate prostitution, just to stream it into an acceptable level of invisibility. The more invisible the mode of prostitution, the higher the costs for both customer and prostitute. Poor working women who don't have their own places or their own phones, or enough money to advertise, find it impossible to work indoors. Residents' groups and police boards don't call for the release of the names of men busted in whorehouses, but they do periodically call for the release of the names of men busted during street sweeps. More hypocrisy, and it doesn't stop there.

When you think about it, men buy sex from strange women all the time but few of the women are prostitutes. A man who patronizes a night club and spends a couple of hundred dollars on a woman he just met earlier in the evening makes his intentions pretty clear — he wants to take her to bed. The man has broken no law by attempting to seduce her, regardless of how much he spends in the process. If this same man walks to the corner of Jarvis and Gerrard streets, hands fifty dollars to a hooker and says, "Let's go," he's committing a crime. Why? The woman in the club can refuse the man's advances; so can the hooker on the corner. The man may abuse the prostitute, but he may also abuse the woman from the night club. The prostitute may have been actively soliciting sex, but so might the woman in the club — they may even dress alike.

Prostitutes have been branded harbingers of the street drug trade but bars and night clubs are excellent places to find illegal drugs. Club owners know that if they attract women to their establishments by offering discount incentives such as Ladies' Nights, the men, many of whom buy and sell illegal drugs, will follow. Have barflies inadvertently become cheerleaders for the drug trade? If the presence of prostitutes on a street conveys the message to men cruising by that all the women in the neighbourhood are available for hire, what message is conveyed by the women who dress up in expensive hooker drag and hang around outside of popular clubs? Although the similarities between the commercial and the casual sex scenes are numerous and obvious, the men who choose the former over the latter become criminals and scourges of neighbourhoods, even though night clubs and bars are attracting a more violent crowd and becoming more dangerous, perhaps more dangerous than any street corner.

In the spring of 1992, when my partner and I were in Amsterdam to present a paper on prostitution and safer-sex education at the Eighth International Conference on AIDS, we learned of a Dutch organization formed by clients of prostitutes. The organization's purpose was to act as a voice for the customers of prostitutes, and to support the Dutch prostitutes' rights organization, The Red Thread. The Dutch whores I spoke with all dismissed the client group, describing it as an organization of one — a customer who had a thing for whores. While I suspected my Dutch peers were right, I couldn't help thinking there was a need for a clients' advocacy group in Canada. Chances are I'll never see one.

chapter 4

Let Your Fingers
Do the Walking

In the business of prostitution all kinds of paraphernalia are used — provocative clothing and make-up, condoms, and a few basic sex toys such as a vibrator, dildos and a good strap — but these items are only trappings. There are two things essential to a working call-girl: a sense of humour and a telephone.

The telephone links customers to working women. A sense of humour allows working women to keep on working. Telephone numbers for escort agencies and independent call-girls are found in the Yellow Pages (Toronto the Good's phone book includes more than thirty pages of escort and call-girl ads) or in the back pages of entertainment newspapers. Daily papers carry ads placed by prostitutes in the classified sections, but when it comes to prostitution, the editors of our dailies don't believe in truth in advertising. Hooker ads have to be camouflaged so as to appear non-commercial. When I see an ad that reads, "Single woman seeks generous gent for discreet encounters," or "Young woman seeks established men for casual good times," I suspect that the person placing the ad is trolling for customers. Words such as "generous," "established" or "financially secure" are obvious giveaways, as are the key words "discreet" and "casual." It's perfectly legal for prostitutes to advertise in newspapers and magazines but many publications will not knowingly accept ads from prostitutes. During my last few years in the Biz, *The Toronto Star* tried to purge hooker ads from its personal classified section. Ironically, the Torstar Corporation, publishers of *The Star*, financially supports *eye Weekly*, the entertainment tabloid which features pages of explicit ads placed by prostitutes, strip clubs, phone sex operators and others involved in Toronto's sex industry.

Weekly entertainment tabloids carry hundreds of very flagrant prostitution ads. In Toronto, *eye* and *NOW*, as well as the twice-monthly gay tabloid, *Xtra!*, carry ads which cater to almost every conceivable sexual taste. The bulk of these ads are poorly written and leave nothing to the reader's imagination. From time to time these publications are criticized for publishing "such filth" and in 1990 the Metro Toronto Police went so far as to charge the publishers and senior editors of *NOW* magazine with communicating for the purpose of prostitution. *NOW* won the court case and the ads remained.

Both *NOW* and *eye* have two rates for their personal classifieds — one for adult service ads, such as those placed by prostitutes, and another, much lower rate, for those placed by people trying to unload fridges and clunker cars. When I was advertising my services in these publications, I asked why we were charged more for our advertising. I was told the hooker ads were difficult to administrate because the advertisers often refused to pay up on overdue accounts. My suggestion to charge prostitutes the same rates as everyone else, but collect the fees in advance, was politely declined. It is clear that Toronto's entertainment tabloids are joined at the hip to the sex trade; these ads earn them a great deal of money.

While many ads are very graphic, the only important piece of information they contain are phone numbers. Funky names such as Sabrina or Victoria, wordy physical descriptions, or erotic explanations of what the women will do are all a waste of money and print. Judging by the wide variety of calls I received during every working day, the eager customers don't bother reading the text of the ads — they just see the phone number and start dialling. Many, too many, just want free sex.

*   *   *

It's four in the morning. My telephone starts ringing. I answer with a sleep-laden, grumpy, "Hello…"

A low male voice, trying to sound sexy, says, "Did I wake you?" I wonder how many people he thinks are awake at four in the morning.

"Yes," I answer, still grumpy, still sleep-laden.

"I'm sorry," he says.

No you're not. "So, what do you want?"

"My name's Jim. Can we talk?"

These guys always use such boring aliases. "Sure Jim, what do you want to talk about?"

"What's your name?"

"Alex, what's yours? Oh, never mind — it's Jim, right?"

"Huh? Yeah, Jim, my name's Jim."

"Okay Jim, why are you calling me at" — I check the glowing red numbers on my bedside clock radio — "four in the morning?"

"I saw your ad in the paper and I thought I'd call you up. I'm laying here in bed with nothing on and …"

"I don't do phone sex for free, Jim. Goodbye." As I hang up I can hear him asking me what I'm wearing.

I click on my answering machine. Jim will call back, guaranteed. Or — and these calls aren't rare enough either — some religious nut will dial me up and tell me how I'll fry in hell because prostitution is a mortal sin. My phone rings. The message tape plays and instructs the caller to leave a telephone number if he wants me to return the call. It's Jim. He tells me he knows I'm there and he begins to describe a certain piece of his anatomy. I pick up the receiver then drop it back into its cradle, cutting him off in mid-pant. I turn the volume down on my machine and shut off the ringer on the phone. Jim can call to his heart's content but I won't hear a thing. As I sink back into the pillow I watch a tiny red light flash on the machine — he's trying again.

*   *   *

An old whore once told me I had to get fifty calls a day to turn one trick. She was right. People who left phone numbers got their messages returned but more often than not these calls led nowhere. Between the time the message was left and I returned the call the potential customer would sober up, find someone else, or change his mind. The answering machine proved most useful as a way to weed out weirdos, but it was also a good way to hook new customers. I could let the caller talk for a while on tape and when I was sure it was legit, I could pick up the receiver. That's what happened with Hans.

He called me in the middle of the night and was looking for a very specific service. "I want someone who is strong, someone who can hit hard," he said.

"I can hit hard when someone wants me to." I had seen plenty of fetishists who had unusual requests and this was not the strangest.

"How tall are you?" he asked. I noticed just a touch of apprehension in his voice.

"Six feet." I was in transition at this point (1989); physically I was more male than female, but I was living as a woman. I considered it important to be upfront with my clients about it — they needed to know what kind of person they'd be seeing. As it turned out though, Hans wasn't interested in the details of my transition; in fact my gender didn't seem to be at all important to him.

"You're very tall and I bet you can hit hard. Tall people can put a lot of energy into their blows."

Bingo, I had him hooked. I could tell by the sound of his voice that he was interested in seeing me and now he was preparing himself to ask the question.

"And how much do you charge for your, ah … talents?"

There was just the right amount of caution in his voice. Men who sound really forward and confident are often not serious about going through with a date — they'd rather play games — or they're cops trying to sound like customers.

"That depends on what you want to do and how long you want to be with me. Time is money." I hated discussing actual dollar figures but I always wanted new customers to know they were dealing with a pro.

"We would not be together long." he said. "There would be no sex. I want to do something else."

"We start negotiating at $150 an hour, so long as there's no sex. If you change your mind the rates change."

"That's fine. Now, I want to meet with you beforehand, for a coffee. I'm sure you understand. After, if I like you, we go to your place — agreed?"

"Yes, but there's a refusal fee of fifty dollars if you change your mind. If I change my mind the meeting costs nothing."

The refusal fee could be a touchy thing for many customers but I always mentioned it. I wanted the customer to know *I* was serious, even if *he* wasn't. Most of my refusals did pay me something, which offset the time and money spent on wild-goose chases. This fellow agreed, which I took as another good sign, because most clients who agreed to the refusal fee didn't refuse the call.

"We can meet in the coffee shop at Pape and Danforth. My name is Hans and I'll be wearing a blue security guard's uniform. I'll be easy to recognize because I'm the only guard who goes in there at seven in the morning."

"Seven ... you want to meet me at seven in the morning?" Surprise was obvious in my voice.

"Yes. I'll explain when I see you. I take it you live somewhere downtown, so after we have coffee I'll drive us to your address. There's parking?"

"Yes, parking's no problem. So when do you want to do this?"

"Why, this morning of course." He sounded surprised that I asked what seemed to me a very logical question. "Why, wait, unless you've already made plans for the morning?"

"No, none."

"Good. It's settled then. I'll see you at seven."

"Okay … Hey, I never told you how to recognize me."

"Oh," he laughed, "you'll be easy to spot. You'll be the one who looks totally out of place. And don't get dressed up. I want you to look rough, like you just rolled out of bed."

That's easy, I thought. "All right then, I'll see you in the morning." He hung up. I called him back, using the number he gave me, and confirmed everything. I set the alarm on my clock radio for six in the morning, turned off the sound on my answering machine, and went to bed. I had five hours of sleep ahead of me and I wanted it all.

I walked into Hans's designated coffee shop at seven on the nose. The place was full of men, all dressed in well-worn work clothes. I concluded that the bleary-eyed ones were all going home while the bright-eyed guys were going to work. There was one blue-clad security guard sitting with his back to me at the coffee bar. He was short and looked to be barrel-chested. His close-cropped black hair was thinning, but at least he wasn't trying to hide his progressing baldness with a baseball cap. Not too vain. I went over and sat down next to him. We exchanged glances of recognition; he bought me a coffee, then we moved to a quiet table.

Over coffee Hans told me a bit about himself. He was a single man who lived alone and worked two jobs: accounting by day and security by night. He spoke quietly and deliberately and his German accent was barely discernible. I enjoy European accents, so I asked what was happening to his. He explained that he had lived in Canada for over ten years.

He said I was what he was looking for. My hands appeared to fascinate him. He was pleased that the skin was smooth and my long nails carefully manicured. He wanted me to use my hands to spank his bare bottom the way an angry parent would spank a bad child. I agreed to do this for $150.

During the drive to my apartment Hans explained why he saw prostitutes first thing in the morning. His day job ended in the late afternoon or early evening and then he'd have a sleep before starting his security job at midnight. There he sat behind a desk and watched surveillance monitors until six in the morning. For Hans, a visit to a whore first thing in the morning was similar to a stockbroker's "nooner" — both men got their jollies in the middle of their working days.

Whenever Hans got into the mood to see a whore, he called hookers who advertised in the entertainment tabloids. Pros willing to accommodate his unusual schedule were rare, so he was thrilled to find me. Hans was a very polite customer and treated my apartment with respect. He removed his shoes at the door, hung up his coat, and asked permission before doing anything. Many submissive clients act like this as part of their scene, but Hans did it because he was well mannered. Once he had made himself comfortable, I collected my fee. He then undressed and insisted I do the same.

I sat in a high-backed chair and he lay face down over my knees. He wanted me to spank his bare bottom twenty times, as hard as I could. "I want you to make my cheeks cherry red," he said, and I did so in twenty good whacks. He never cried out. After I heated up his butt, we changed positions.

I allowed him to spank me but only very lightly — I wasn't into pain, and bruises weren't good for business. He never showed any sign of arousal during his scene but said he thoroughly enjoyed the experience. Once the session was over, he quickly got dressed while chatting with me and fussing over my cat. He then left, promising to call again. I saw Hans often and our dates always followed this routine.

Hans was one of only a very small number of customers that I let strike me. Many prostitutes would flatly refuse to see someone like Hans, but I trusted him right from the beginning. I felt he would always respect my limits, however I set them, and he never surprised me. In prostitution surprises can be dangerous and I never encouraged or tolerated them with any of my customers.

It was great to make $150 cash before breakfast, but early birds like Hans were very rare. I spent most workday mornings doing housework and getting my apartment (or trick pad) ready for the afternoon and evening business.

My cat had a ritual she went through whenever I brought home a new customer. At the beginning of the date Sabbath would disappear but stay within earshot. If she came out of hiding while the new client and I discussed the date and money, I knew everything would happen according to plan. My black-and-white trick barometer was never wrong. Sabbath took to Hans right away so I knew he was cool. Many of my customers, including Hans, reacted well to Sabbath; they saw me as being more like a regular person, and easier to relate to, because I had such an ordinary pet. It made it easier for clients to call on me again.

Another customer who sometimes disrupted my morning routine was the Tooth Fairy. Tooth would call me around nine, usually when the weather was horrible. He always made arrangements to see me at eleven o'clock at his home. My appearance was important to him — he insisted I looked my best — so he gave me those two hours to get ready. I'd fuss up then catch a cab to the Tooth Fairy's digs, a Victorian reno in the Queen and Bathurst area of Toronto.

Tooth always came to the door dressed in an old bathrobe. Once inside, the routine never varied. He'd take my coat and invite me into his living room. The living room, like all the rooms in the house, was dark and cluttered but seemed clean. Above the fireplace, which looked unused, the mantel supported an array of trophies, awards for school athletics, and other odds and ends. Every flat surface in the room held some small collection of things; brass figurines, sea shells, glass balls containing little scenes — the kind that simulate snow storms when you shake them. Newspapers and magazines were scattered all over the couches and chairs. Drapes covered the windows, heightening the behind-closed-doors nature of what we were about to do. My fee — a cool two hundred dollars — would be where it always was whenever I visited Tooth, in plain view on a curio table. A neat stack of ten twenty-dollar bills. Always the same amount, always offered up the same way. Such organization in such a disorganized setting.

Tooth Fairy wasn't a bad sort, but I couldn't smoke in his house, so I didn't waste time on small talk. We exchanged pleasantries, then went upstairs to Tooth's bedroom. The room looked as if it belonged to a child who dreamed of becoming a dentist. Hand-drawn dental maps of the mouths of Tooth's former lovers adorned one wall, flanking one of his prize possessions — a dental X-ray of someone's mouth.

A small bookcase held well-thumbed dental textbooks filled with photos of bad and broken teeth, as well as before-and-after pictures of the work done by dental surgeons. Dental implements — little round mirrors, hooks and probes — were scattered about the rumpled bed and laid out on a bedside table.

When I first met the Tooth Fairy I thought I had heard about every kind of fetish going but Tooth was unique — he was turned on by teeth and he liked imperfections. He enjoyed seeing me because I had a chipped tooth and cavities. Whenever I visited him, I sat on the bed facing him, with my legs crossed and my mouth open. He probed and poked around my mouth with a pick, much like a real dentist, except that the pick was plastic, not the real thing. (I wouldn't allow him to use a real instrument.) As he did so, he questioned me about my dental history, but I soon learned not to tell the Tooth Fairy too much — he preferred making his own discoveries about changes to my teeth. I often noticed a hint of disappointment in his voice when he found improvements had been made.

I didn't have to do anything *to* the Tooth Fairy. He just wanted me to sit there and let him look in my mouth. The date was very easy once I got past thinking about how weird it all was. I saw the Tooth Fairy many times and whenever I did I always employed one of the standard hooker defences against weirdness — I sat there and thought about the money.

As he poked and prodded, he became more and more aroused, until, suddenly, he would excuse himself and disappear into the bathroom. After a few minutes, he'd reappear, escort me to the door and bid me a good day. His dates always ended abruptly.

I didn't question the Tooth Fairy about his strange fetish. He was a harmless man who posed no threat, a totally predictable customer who paid well, and that was all I needed to know.

Over a period of two years or so I saw Tooth at least two dozen times, but eventually I lost him as a customer. During this time I had thousands of dollars' worth of real dental work done. A talented dentist replaced all my old fillings, filled new cavities and capped the chipped tooth. Once all the imperfections and rough edges were gone, Tooth Fairy stopped calling me.

Movies and popular fiction usually depict prostitutes whiling away their days making themselves more beautiful for their fabulously wealthy clients, or getting stoned. Pros are rarely shown cleaning house, buying groceries, hanging out with friends, or just sitting around waiting for the damn phone to ring. These ordinary activities took up most of my days. It was important to me to have my work place, be it my apartment or my trick pad, looking good. I wanted my customers to feel that my place was always clean and fresh — just ready and waiting for them. But once the last customer of the day had gone all vestiges of work were removed and my apartment was once again my home. I never slept on dirty sheets.

Prostitution is not a lifestyle or an adventure — it's a job. I liked having a social life outside the Business and feeling connected to the more traditional world where people led ordinary lives. I needed to feel grounded in normalcy, to be in touch with regular day-to-day activities. I read all the local newspapers and watched the news every night. I chatted with total strangers in bars and coffee shops. I wrote long (albeit infrequent) letters to my parents.

The bulk of my trade was in the afternoon and early evening. Hans was my only sun-up regular and I loathed seeing customers after midnight. I found that the later the hour, the more likely it was that the trick would be drunk or high. I had a rule about not seeing men who were impaired. Drunk men often get argumentative and refuse to pay the going rate. If they can't perform because of their impairment, they blame it on the pro. Drunks can also be violent. They just aren't worth the trouble. On the other hand, afternooners were always sober, prompt, and knew exactly what they wanted. These men were well-behaved and easy to handle.

Among prostitutes, British customers, particularly older ones, have a reputation for being into classic kink: sadomasochism, bondage and domination, rubber and latex, or transvestism. The Englishman who saw my ad and called me up was no exception. He asked if I had done much work with people who were into rubber. I hadn't. Would I? Sure. Did I own any rubber gear? Nope. No problem, he'd provide the outfits. Outfits!? He took my size and dimensions over the phone. He also asked me if I would masturbate him if he wore a condom. Of course. I was pleased to hear that this customer was concerned about disease transmission and took the initiative in advocating safe sex practices. I didn't know it at the time, but his insistence on condom use had nothing to do with safe sex.

The Englishman showed up at my door a couple of hours after our first conversation. He was in his fifties or early sixties, tall, stiff-backed and very well dressed. He had that polished look that comes from living in a well-ordered, affluent world. He carried a large box which bore the label of a well-known sporting-goods store.

After we took care of the financial aspects of the date, he opened the box and produced two pairs of green rubber hip waders and two matching rubber coats. One outfit looked somewhat worn, while the other was brand new. The old rubber suit was his, and he took it into the bathroom and shut the door. From there he called out to me, telling me to put on the new outfit. I slipped off my dressing gown and put on the hip waders and jacket over my bra and panties. I had never worn rubber clothes before and found the outfit hot and heavy. The strong rubber smell was overpowering.

When the Englishman came out of the bathroom, all dressed up in rubber, he looked me up and down and gave me an approving smile. I felt ridiculous. The hip waders were far too big and the jacket hung on me like a bedsheet. The Englishman came towards me, took me in his arms and kissed me hard on the mouth. His hands were all over me — hugging, squeezing, stroking and caressing. I felt beads of sweat forming on my back, not from passion but because of the hot, silly costume. I leaned back and let the jacket slip off me while my date nuzzled his face between my small breasts. He then produced a bright red condom and slipped it on. The condom wasn't being used to protect either of us from STDs; he just liked the feel of the snug latex.

"Tell me how disgusting this all is," he demanded. "Tell me you think this is filthy. Make it sound real."

I didn't expect him to be into verbal abuse and I wished he had warned me in advance. I have plenty of experience dishing out abuse to submissive clients, and some said I was quite good at it, but I needed time to psych myself up. Hurling streams of abuse at a stranger is not as easy to do as it may sound, especially when you're doing it because the target has asked you to. The voice and the words become sex toys and, like any adult toy, you've got to know how to use it to get the most out of it.

I began cajoling and berating him and to add a little emphasis to my performance I stepped out of the too-big hip waders and kicked them across the floor. I continued to tell the Englishman just what a disgusting, perverted creature he was until he was satisfied and collapsed onto my bed. While he caught his breath, I gathered up the rubber clothes I had scattered about the room and placed them back in the box. I opened my balcony door and the fresh air felt delicious against my clammy, overheated skin.

My date offered me a cigarette, a Dunhill — British to the end. We sat and smoked while he told me how much fun he had. He also told me he had a lover, a much younger man, who just couldn't tolerate the rubber and domination fetish. The lover knew the Englishman was seeing prostitutes but didn't mind. I saw him about once a month, for over a year. I enjoyed seeing him, not because I cared much for the sex (I still hate the smell of rubber), but because I thoroughly enjoyed our après-sex conversations. The Englishman was an intelligent, sensitive man involved in a loving relationship that accommodated unconventional practices. My only regret was that I never met his lover!

One of my favourite customers was Hal. When he first called, I was intrigued by the way he handled himself over the phone and I liked the sound of his voice. We arranged to meet the next day at the patio bar of the Isabella Hotel.

On the day of our meeting I dressed carefully. I wanted to appear tasteful, so I wore a classically simple cream-coloured silk blouse over light casual slacks. My outfit could've taken me anywhere and I was ready for anything.

The Isabella Hotel was a short walk from my apartment building. As I approached the hotel's patio I saw Hal sitting alone under a large umbrella festooned with beer ads. He had very pale blond hair and wore a neatly trimmed beard; his clothes were fashionable and summery. He recognized me almost as soon as I saw him and rose when I approached his table. Hal was gracious and chatty through lunch but he revealed little about himself.

Towards the end of our meal we began to discuss prostitution and that led to the subject of my transition. Being in transition was both a blessing and a curse throughout most of my career in prostitution. Many clients saw me as something exotic, a walk on the wild side. Others saw me as a gentle introduction to gay sex — I was sort of a man in their eyes but not quite, so they could sort of have gay sex with me, but not quite. If they enjoyed themselves but got hung up over the idea of "turning gay" they could rationalize their fears away by telling themselves that I was in the process of becoming a woman, which, in their minds, made everything okay. If they didn't enjoy their time with me, they could at least walk away thinking they were true-blue heterosexual.

Hal was fascinated. He was curious as to why someone would choose to change from being a member of the advantaged sex to become a member of the disadvantaged. Hal's interest seemed thoughtful and genuine, and I answered all of his questions as openly and honestly as I could.

We arranged a date for later that night and before I left the patio, Hal gave me a demure kiss on the cheek and whispered how much he looked forward to our upcoming appointment. I shared his enthusiasm. I felt better after my meeting with Hal than I had felt in months. I seldom had the opportunity to really explain transition to anyone, and it was rare for anyone to understand and accept what I said the way Hal had. He treated me like a lady — without hesitation. Our luncheon had gone well, and I felt the evening could only be better. I spent the rest of the afternoon wandering around the neighbourhood window shopping and daydreaming, trying to guess what Hal wanted to do when he saw me as a whore.

I usually put a lot of work into getting ready for a client but I went all out preparing to see Hal, a man who already knew more about me than friends who had known me for years. I wanted him to find me erotically attractive but I also wanted him to find me attractive simply as a woman. I dressed in my classiest lingerie and my hair and make-up were as close to perfect as I could get them. My appearance pleased me; I hoped it would please him.

When Hal arrived at my apartment I knew I had succeeded. He wasn't sure how long he wanted to stay with me, but he paid me four hundred dollars up front and made it clear that he had more cash in reserve. He didn't want to feel pressed for time, he explained, and I certainly had no plans to pressure him. We quickly got down to the business at hand, and I soon realized that Hal was a skilled, sensitive lover.

We saw one another two or three times a month for almost three years, until he moved to Montreal. He quickly became the standard against whom I compared all my other dates.

Hal was married and had a family — a family he professed to love very much. He and his wife had been together for over twenty years and Hal had no intention of threatening the marriage. To him I was a sexual diversion, a plaything not to be taken too seriously. He made it clear that our relationship would always be a professional one and that suited me just fine. Outside of my apartment Hal had to remain a stranger; if I saw him on the street, I couldn't show any sign of recognition. Our luncheon at the Isabella never happened, nor could it ever again. I agreed to his terms. He promised he would treat me as well as I treated him, but he did more than that. He often called me just to see how I was doing, and whenever we got together he treated me like a queen. Hal became one of a small number of clients whom I truly missed between dates.

Clients like Hal make such a difference to people working in prostitution. He made it clear that he considered me a talented professional. He was generous with his money but, more importantly, he respected and accepted me. If only there were more like him.

After turning a long, involved date, such as one with Hal, I would close up shop, pick up around the house and either take a shower or a long hot bath. When I was a child my mother would send me to the tub on a Sunday night, after which, all wet and squeaky clean, I would crawl under a small, heavy mountain of freshly laundered covers and fall asleep in minutes. Going to bed as an adult prostitute was slightly more involved. Did I want to deal with live callers at three in the morning? No. Off would go my answering machine's speaker and the ringer on the phone — if I'd had a good day I wouldn't want it marred by horny insomniacs. I'd probably set my clock radio for ten the next morning.

Perhaps I'd think about paying some bills the next day or treating myself to something. Finally, all wet and squeaky clean, I would crawl under a small, heavy mountain of blankets, and fall asleep in minutes.

chapter 5

Red, White
and Blue

B ack in 1973, I noticed that as I walked along the quieter
streets in Toronto's downtown core cars often slowed
down as they passed by, the drivers checking me out. Some
smiled as they cruised by, most just looked then drove on.
My heart always beat faster whenever I sensed someone
checking me out through his windshield. By the latter part
of my first winter in the city I felt I could step out onto the
street and make some quick money. I thought this would
free me from the whims of David's friends and open up a
whole new aspect of prostitution to me.

Once I decided to take my business outside I was confronted with a serious dilemma — where do I work?
Although I felt more feminine than masculine I still looked
masculine and I didn't think the women working downtown
would appreciate my company. I settled on Toronto's male
stroll, Boystown, which was composed of a half-dozen or so

grey streets bordered by Wellesley to the north, College to the south, Yonge to the east and Queen's Park to the west. The stroll encircles parking lots and drab office towers and is anchored by Metro Police headquarters on College Street. Most of the area's daytime pedestrians were Bay Streeters rushing around trying to find an upscale eatery; at night virtually no one walked around the stroll unless they were planning to buy or sell sex. Much of Boystown is in sight of the Ontario Legislature and other lesser provincial government buildings; I didn't know it at the time but it's common in many Canadian cities for the male stroll to be located close to government buildings. I walked through Boystown often before testing the waters and I was sized up every time. Guys in cars eyed me up and down as they tried to figure out whether I was working or just walking. Young male whores checked me out in an effort to determine whether I was a customer or a competitor. I found the attentions of the drivers exciting but the watchful gazes of the hustlers troubled me. Many of the boys looked rough in their sprayed-on jeans and half-open bomber jackets, lurking in the shadows like extras from *West Side Story*. Often, only clouds of exhaled cigarette smoke gave away their locations. No one hassled me though; in fact the only time any of the Boystown whores even approached me was to bum cigarettes. No one seemed drunk or high and no one looked like they could produce two nickels to rub together. I couldn't help but wonder why anyone would want to be out here — but then again I could have asked myself the same question.

When whores are working they're not walking and I found a quiet corner and tried to make myself comfortable while remaining visible. Car after car cruised up Bay Street without any of the drivers giving me so much as a second look. I smoked one cigarette after another, imagining the butts piling up and covering my feet while I waited for something to happen.

Cars, cars, cars, then finally one stopped. It was a little box on wheels, an Escort or Chevette with no guts and no room. How could I turn somebody in a thing like that? The driver was male, probably under forty, ordinary looking. He called to me. I walked over and leaned into the open passenger window — the classic street hooker stance.

"Where can a guy like me find a good time?" he asked nervously, trying to smile.

I took in the key ring hanging from the car's ignition, smelled the Old Spice. Keys, a miniature pen knife, other junk — probably not a rented car. In those days I thought that was a good sign. City of Toronto map on the passenger seat. Even better. "That depends on what a guy like you likes to do." I flashed my professional smile. "Are you willing to spend some money?"

"Sure am," he said, filling in his grin. "Get in and tell me just how much money we're talking about."

"Now that depends," I said as I slid into the passenger seat of the car, "on what you have in mind. Head will run you fifty dollars."

The driver frowned and shook his head. "You should know better."

I looked the driver in the eye. His grin was gone. "Do I know you?"

"Not personally," he said, "But you should've been able to make me for what I am." He reached into a jacket pocket and withdrew what looked like a credit card holder. He opened it up and I saw the badge.

"Shit."

"Yeah, shit. What are you doing out here?" The cop's voice had instantly become more severe. He didn't sound threatening but he meant business.

"Killing time; it's a nice night."

"So why'd you try to trick me like I was some dumb tourist?"

"Because you looked like some dumb tourist and you acted like some dumb tourist." I sighed, thinking I'd get a summons and have to pay a fine. "And it's my job."

"Your job," the cop scoffed. "Bullshit! I've never seen you out here."

"I don't work out here. I work indoors, through ads." He looked at me hard, trying to determine whether to believe me. The cop lit a cigarette, then offered me one, which I took.

"And you should," agreed the cop. "This shit," he waved his hand across the windshield of his car, "is for losers. The street's no place for a professional and if you've got to hook you should at least work like a pro. I'm not going to bother busting you. Go home and listen to your damn answering machine."

"Yeah, thanks." I looked at him, my professional smile gone. I have no idea why, but the police officer had given me a break. "You won't see me down here again." My short career on the street was over.

*   *   *

Prostitutes have always said that it's difficult to get the police to act on their complaints about rough customers and other violent types. In 1989, when I began meeting a lot of pros, the general opinion was, "Why go to the cops, they won't do anything." Prostitutes felt they were on their own when it came to dealing with robberies and violence. They also felt they risked getting charged with prostitution offences if they went to the police to complain about bad dates, abusive pimps or other dangerous men. Few men were charged and punishments were little more than slaps on wrists. This has finally started to change, albeit slowly. Since society has begun taking the problem of violence against women more seriously, more men have been charged and punished for committing crimes against prostitutes, and the punishments have become more severe. Many whores still argue that the police ignore their complaints, and they often have personal stories to back up their arguments, but it is no longer acceptable for the police and court officials to say things like, "It's not possible to rape a prostitute."

Since the nineteenth century, when the idea of a civilian police force was conceived in England by Sir Robert Peel, cops have had a relationship with prostitutes. Cops and hookers work the same hours, often in the same parts of town and, at times, they deal with the same people. In Peel's day cops were paid little money and many Londoners resented the idea of being watched over by an independent police force. These days coppers often sing the financial blues and say they don't get enough support and cooperation from the general public. So cops and hookers have two more things in common; their work is underpaid and undervalued.

In the cat-and-mouse game of police versus prostitutes the cops are the cats and, like the four-legged predators, they hold all the advantages. Prostitutes who work on the street are more vulnerable; careful indoor whores have much less to worry about. Thanks to telephone services such as call display and call return (both of which show the number the call is being made from) and reverse directories (which list names and addresses according to telephone numbers), the police really have to work hard to bust an escort service or an independent. As the public money pool dries up and budgets get slashed, the police are being forced to spend their limited resources on more important matters than indoor prostitution, but sometimes they do try.

During my last year in the Biz I received call after call from a guy phoning from a 777 exchange in Toronto. Each time the fellow called, he asked about different things — different sexual services, different costumes (he was fond of black and white because he often asked if I owned a French maid's outfit — I didn't), different rates and different times. He also tried to pass himself off as different people, but all the calls came from the same number. When I called this number, a friendly female voice told me I had dialled the Metro Police Special Intelligence Service, the 1990s euphemism for, among other things, the morality squad. I had never knowingly turned a cop and I wasn't about to start by seeing one who called from the office.

An escort who plays the game by the rules laid out in the Criminal Code doesn't have to worry about getting busted but she may suffer financially. A customer who does not invite a whore to his own home, or spring for a hotel room on top of paying for the date, will likely shop around until he finds a woman who does in-calls. Sooner or later everyone who is serious about making money in this business ends up doing in-calls and that's when they run the risk of getting busted if they're not careful. As any woman who has ever placed any kind of a classified ad in a newspaper can tell you, screening calls is crucial. It's also simple. Whenever a client called me, I'd make a note of the displayed phone number as we chatted. Once the niceties were dispensed with, I'd ask the caller what his telephone number was and I'd tell him I would call him right back. If he was reluctant to go through this procedure, I simply explained that I had to screen all of my calls in order to weed out the nuts and the cops. Most legitimate clients were more than willing to cooperate. If the number the caller gave me matched the number on my call display, he passed the first hurdle. If I had doubts about the guy, I quickly rang the local library and asked them to check the phone number for me in their reverse directory. This would provide me with a name and address, and sometimes even an occupation. If I still had doubts about a caller, I told him that an in-call was out of the question. That way, I knew I wasn't running the risk of getting arrested.

Thanks to tips, complaints from residents, or from prostitutes who had been assaulted or ripped off by agency owners, the police have shut down some escort services and busted individual call-girls. These raids and arrests are few and far between, and because of this they attract more than their fair share of media attention. For every escort service that gets put out of business by the police there are literally hundreds of small one- or two-woman operations in a city like Toronto just waiting to pick up a little extra business. As Valerie Scott of the Canadian Organization for the Rights of Prostitutes (CORP) has said so many times, "Toronto has hundreds of small brothels quietly doing business all over the city, in every neighbourhood, in every borough."

The vast majority of prostitution-related arrests stem from street prostitution and most of those arrested are the women, not the clients. Entrapment is standard operating procedure for the police. Cops pose either as hookers to bust customers or as customers to bust hookers and a prostitution sweep of a neighbourhood can last two or three nights. During the first night or two the police try to charge as many pros as they can net; on the last night they go after the customers. One evening I watched the Metro Police run a john sting; a young female officer, dressed in a denim miniskirt and shorty jacket, snagged as many unlucky customers as she and her two male back-up officers could process. She was far more aggressive in her solicitations than any real hooker I've ever watched, but the clueless customers didn't notice the difference. The phony pro strutted, winked, waved and whistled as the unsuspecting lined up to receive their summonses. (A real pro would have stood around, waiting to be approached by customers.) I realized that if the police wanted to, and if they had the resources, they could bust hundreds of customers a week in Toronto — but what point would it serve? The men who tired of street roulette and had money would eventually start phoning escorts. Prostitution wouldn't be eliminated, it would just go underground and become more of a diversion for the rich.

The street is the birthplace of as many myths as rumours. Most of these myths are supposed to keep people out of the courts and ultimately out of jail but, like most misinformation, they do the opposite. Many prostitutes I have met believed the easiest way to foil undercover cops working a hooker sweep was to grab their crotches as soon as they got into the cars, or invite them to fondle their breasts.

They were under the impression that cops wouldn't, or couldn't, fondle the pros or allow the pros to fondle them. Contrary to myth, a cop's investigation is not compromised if he is fondled by a prostitute. If he agrees to do the groping after a pro insists — and her comments are recorded on tape — it's difficult for the woman to successfully charge him with sexual assault. A plainclothes cop has a certain amount of leeway in setting his trap and it's unlikely a bust would be tossed out of court unless the methods used to entrap the prostitutes brought the criminal justice system into disrepute. If a narcotics officer peddled crack cocaine to a group of school children then busted them all for possession, his actions would bring the system into disrepute. If a cop working a sweep allows a prostitute to touch him — anywhere — that likely would not. It hasn't yet.

Another myth was that a pro couldn't be busted if all the business was negotiated while she still had one foot on the sidewalk. Not true. Communicating in public is communicating in public. Some women make a big deal over keys and key rings. "Get out of cars that only have one or two keys on the rings. They're rental cars and cops use rental cars on sweeps because cop cars are so easy to spot." Well, tourists use rental cars too and tourists can be good customers because they're often loose with money.

Prostitutes dislike cops for more than just the obvious reason. Many people claim the police treat women differently than men, and that they treat prostitutes as a different class of woman — regardless of the nature of the interaction. In the summer of 1991 a woman was found dead in a garage located on a street near Toronto's Cabbagetown stroll. Like a spin doctor on speed the rumour mill began spewing out stories and before long every pro who worked downtown believed a hooker killer was prowling the streets. The police weren't saying anything despite the obvious concern on the stroll. The issue came to a head when my partner Karen and I and a half-dozen street hookers (one pushing her baby in a stroller) walked into 40 College Street and demanded some answers. In front of two uncomfortable-looking female officers the duty sergeant gave us the predictable response; he told us violence came with the territory and if we didn't like it, we should get out of the sex trade. He ignored Karen's attempts to explain that she was a concerned resident, not a prostitute, and he looked at the new mother and her baby with disdain. We stomped out of police headquarters very angry but no better informed. A few days later we learned that the mystery woman had died months earlier, probably of hypothermia. She wasn't a prostitute, as far as anyone knew, and there wasn't a killer stalking the downtown pros. Calm returned to the stroll and business went back to normal. The duty sergeant we spoke to could have done so much to alleviate our fears; he could have told us the police were close to solving the mystery. But he gave us the brush off because he believed we were just a bunch of whores and beneath contempt.

More than AIDS, more than bad dates, prostitutes fear the police. It's not just the fear of arrest that keeps streetwalkers looking over their shoulders; there is a real fear of the police themselves, the rogue cops. In the summer of 1991 *Toronto Star* reporters Andrew Duffy and Sally Ritchie came to me with the idea of doing an exposé of police violence against prostitutes. Everyone in the press had heard stories of these alleged police abuses — extortion, rapes, violence and the infamous Cherry Beach Express.

The reporters wanted to bring all of this to light, but they needed names, places, dates and descriptions of what happened. Duffy and Ritchie wanted me to act as a go-between between them and the downtown hookers, thinking the women might be more willing to talk with the journalists if I vouched for their professional integrity. I was willing to assist, provided *The Star* was willing to take steps to protect the identities of the women who spoke out. *The Star* agreed and Sally Ritchie and I hit the stroll looking for evidence.

Prostitutes are generally suspicious of the media because of the way the press depicts prostitution and those involved in it. Hookers are always portrayed as victims, drug addicts or threats to the sanctity of neighbourhoods. Pros resent the fact that the media seldom shows any respect for their privacy; television crews seem to think nothing of driving through strolls with their cameras rolling, filming prostitutes without their permission and often without their knowledge. The footage inevitably shows up on the evening news while a voice-over describes the horrors of the sex trade. I was afraid Toronto's downtown hookers would refuse to speak with us and send us packing the moment Ritchie identified herself as a journalist. Surprisingly, the floodgates opened; every woman we approached had a story and was eager to tell it. Over and over we heard comments like, "Finally you're coming to us instead of just making up stories about us," or "It's about time someone from the press was willing to take this seriously." We were told of beatings and rapes, robberies and other assaults. A skinny older blonde in a flimsy dress described a vicious assault she suffered at the hands of the police, all the while emphasizing her remarks by waving around a broken right arm. Another woman talked about how it felt to have a gun shoved in her mouth, while yet another told us how a cop made her strip, then run naked into Lake Ontario. Most of the women who talked with us claimed to know the names or the badge numbers of the cops who allegedly assaulted them but no one was willing to give this information to me or Ritchie. The women feared reprisals; they knew the officers involved could identify the talkers by the stories they told and they knew a newspaper's anonymity couldn't protect them. Without the identities of individual police officers *The Star's* story died and the horrific accounts of the prostitutes faded into the night.

One street name — "Sperm Whale" — came up repeatedly while Ritchie and I talked with the women. No one could, or would, identify this cop but he had a reputation for being extremely violent. In *Stiletto*, a newsletter written and distributed on the street during the summer of 1990 by CORP and Maggie's, Sperm Whale was described as "a huge cop ... dangerous.... He forces girls to suck him off, sometimes at gunpoint, and steals their money.... If enough of us complain about Sperm Whale we can get the police department to do something."

In November of 1991 the Metro Toronto Police said they had tried to do something. During an inquiry into the conduct of Metro Police's internal affairs unit, Police Superintendent Aidan Maher said he had known one particular officer for seven years who might fit the description of Sperm Whale. He described him as a dedicated morality cop who "arrested hundreds of prostitutes so he was not a popular man." He went on to say that earlier in 1990 he

directed a team of officers to look into the allegations published in *Stiletto*, but he said the investigation was dropped
because no one was willing to provide the police with information. Not surprising — prostitutes knew the complaints
they made to internal affairs were routinely turned over to
morality officers, the same cops responsible for enforcing
prostitution laws. Maher also suggested that the description
of Sperm Whale published in *Stiletto* could be a composite
of any number of cops. "There could be one Sperm Whale,
there could be twenty-two." Maher's chilling comment begs
the question: was Metro Police Sergeant Brian Whitehead
one of those twenty-two Sperm Whales?

Early in 1989 Whitehead, while off duty but still in
uniform, picked up a woman on a Parkdale stroll (he would
later say that the woman approached him and offered him
sex for money). Whitehead drove the woman to her apartment and there, using the threat of arrest for communicating
for the purpose of prostitution, forced her to have sex. Over
the next three weeks he made several attempts to set up
further meetings with her in the hopes of establishing a relationship. The woman, who became known as Jane Doe
because of her unwillingness to be identified in the news
media, claimed not to be a professional prostitute; she was a
middle-class woman with a straight job. She eventually did
what any middle-class woman might do under these circumstances — she contacted a lawyer, Peter Maloney. Through
Maloney, Doe told her story to internal affairs and gave
them supporting evidence, which included a glass with
Whitehead's fingerprints on it and a recording of his voice
taken from her telephone answering machine. Doe helped
internal affairs gather more evidence by wearing a wire and

allowing them to tap her phone. She also let the police set up a bust in her apartment and, on November 22, Whitehead was arrested in Doe's home by internal affairs detectives Richard Lundy and Donald Caisse. Whitehead was taken to the internal affairs unit where it was determined that he was intoxicated. Caisse and Lundy could not have intended to charge Whitehead; he wasn't fingerprinted, no information was sworn against him, no arrest report was filed and no Crown brief was prepared. Three hours later he was sent home. He was not suspended from the police force.

The next day Caisse and Lundy went to work on Whitehead's behalf. They spoke with assistant Crown attorney Uriel Priwes and advised him not to lay criminal charges against Whitehead because there were conflicting statements and no corroborating evidence — an obvious lie. They also tried to present Doe as an unreliable witness. Internal affairs decided not to press criminal charges but instead chose to prosecute Whitehead under the Police Services Act, a course of action usually taken when a police officer commits a non-criminal offence. Because Whitehead admitted he was an alcoholic and voluntarily entered a rehabilitation program, internal affairs felt his punishment should be lenient. They suggested that if Whitehead pleaded guilty to Police Act offences, a short suspension with loss of pay would be good enough. Doe was furious when she heard about the deal cooked up by the police and continued to insist that Whitehead be charged as a criminal and dismissed from the force.

Whitehead's disciplinary hearing took place in May 1990, but Doe was not notified, so she was not present, nor was she represented by counsel. Whitehead kept his part of the bargain and pleaded guilty to Police Act charges of corrupt practice and deceit. Superintendent Duncan Wilson, who presided over the hearing, called Whitehead's actions "a totally despicable abuse of police power and authority." He added, "In my two years as a tribunal officer, I have never had a case before me which depicts so vividly the abuse of power and position of a police officer." Despite these harsh words Wilson's only punishment for Whitehead was demotion, from sergeant to first-class constable.

The Metro Toronto Police faced a storm of criticism over its handling of the Whitehead affair. At the time Roger Hollander, a Metro councillor and a well-known advocate of police reform, wrote, "Chief William McCormack and the Metro Toronto Police Force sent a very clear message out to the women of Toronto. If a cop commits sexual assault or extortion his penalty will be a demotion in rank."

McCormack defended the force and insisted "nothing went wrong" with the case.

I'm sure that Brian Whitehead did what he did to Jane Doe because he believed she was just some dumb hooker. He never tried to cover his tracks; he probably believed Doe had no idea how to work the criminal justice system and didn't have the nerve or the wherewithall to call a lawyer. And if a cop rapes a prostitute, who is she going to call — the police? Not likely. Whitehead probably figured he had nothing to fear and nothing to lose, and he was almost right: he was demoted in rank and took a seven grand a year cut in pay but he remained a cop. Jane Doe was chewed up and spit out.

Despite the actions of officers like Brian Whitehead and the enigmatic Sperm Whale, I don't believe all cops have it out for whores. I suspect most police officers have a rather dispassionate attitude towards prostitutes and I know that many cops feel they shouldn't be policing prostitution at all. I've sat through too many community meetings and talked with too many rank-and-file police officers who have told me they would like to see prostitution decriminalized, or at least legalized, to think otherwise. However, police command officers don't generally support the liberalization of our prostitution laws.

The platform on which the police stand and call for tougher laws is built with only three planks — safety, drugs and organized crime. The women must be protected; prostitution goes hand in hand with the illegal drug trade; and prostitution is linked to organized crime. Whenever a police spokesperson speaks publicly in favour of cracking down on the sex trade, or against the idea of liberalizing Canada's prostitution laws, odds are the officer mentions safety, drugs or gangsters in the same breath. Prostitutes' rights activists have long argued that the police simply don't want to lose a renewable source of arrest statistics.

In April 1993, Ottawa police chief Brian Ford broke ranks and said prostitution should be legalized and regulated because efforts to eliminate it have failed. Ford went on to suggest that the federal government create a task force to go out and talk with prostitutes to find out how they like to work. Ford's position is similar to that of his predecessor Tom Flanagan who, in 1992, said prostitution should be decriminalized. Toronto's chief William McCormack called Ford's ideas ludicrous and showed no concern for the rights and safety of women.

The police cannot protect prostitutes by arresting them and imposing fines or jail time. When judges punish prostitutes by fining them, they're only ensuring that the convicted women must work even harder. Not only do they need the money to pay their fines, but to earn a living. If you exclude work that doesn't pay liveable wages from the total pool of jobs available to prostitutes who wish to leave the trade, the pool dries up. Jailed prostitutes are protected from nothing. Instead, they are given the opportunity to mingle with, and perhaps be influenced by, real criminals while their old lives on the outside crumble. While the women do time, they can lose their children, their homes, perhaps even their lovers and friends. When they get out, they have to rebuild their lives, and the overpowering need for money resurfaces. A criminal record makes it doubly difficult for the women to find traditional employment. The street, or the telephone, is often the only way to satisfy that need.

I don't understand how male police officers can claim that the liberalization of our prostitution laws constitutes an affront to women. The Elizabeth Fry Society, a group which assists women in conflict with the law, has been calling for the decriminalization of prostitution for twenty years, as has every prostitutes' rights group in North America. In the United States NOW, the National Organization of Women, called for decriminalization over twenty years ago, while our own National Action Committee on the Status of Women (NAC) began advocating for decriminalization in the late 1980s. Social service organizations, lesser-known women's groups, health-care organizations, even the Toronto City Council and its mayor, Barbara Hall, have called for decriminalization. Many women's organizations, unlike the high-ranking cops who occasionally feel compelled to speak on their behalf, realized long ago that you don't help prostitutes by fining them repeatedly or tossing them in jail.

For years I've listened to the police say that prostitution and the illegal drug trade are like two sides of the same coin: that women turn to prostitution to support drug habits; that pimps get their whores wired to drugs in order to strengthen their hold on them and make it easier to force the women to work; that dealers hang around hookers and many prostitutes deal drugs to supplement their hooking incomes. This is all true, to a greater or lesser extent. Some prostitutes do work primarily to finance addictions. Pimps have been known to use drugs as addictive carrots in order to better manipulate the whores in their stables. Dealers often do work the same neighbourhoods as prostitutes; they shy away from the police while seeking out high-traffic areas, a necessary element to both prostitution and the drug trade. Street prostitution and street dealing both carry the glamour of quick money, so when we see these activities happening side by side, it's always in poorer neighbourhoods — poverty being the common denominator. Regardless of where the dealers sell their drugs, whether pros use them or what pimps do with them, the police won't affect the drug trade by chasing hookers. Prostitution and drugs must be treated as two different issues.

The majority of prostitutes I met were not drug addicts, they were not even recreational drug users. During my career I encountered every kind of drug user, from heroin addicts to casual marijuana smokers, from all sectors of society. Drug use is the big urban evil of our times. When residents complain about people driving through their neighbourhoods looking for crack dealers, they often talk about the parades of BMWs, Jags and other expensive cars. Staff from needle-exchange programs have told me about well-heeled clients who slink in looking for clean fits. But no one attempts to taint the well-to-do; instead, prostitutes get singled out as ambassadors of drugs and addiction. No wonder the police have lost their war on drugs.

The police tell us if prostitution were decriminalized organized criminals would move in and soon every hooker in town would be working for the mob, a posse or a triad. We are expected to believe that gangsters are just waiting to hop onto the prostitution gravy train. Hookers know this isn't so. Prostitution is a lousy business for organized criminals to get involved in. Mobs, gangs, posses, triads — they all need secrecy and loyal wiseguys to stay in business. Prostitution involves a lot of people and if just one person in the know decides to talk to the police or the press the whole organization can be brought down. In the summer of 1992, *The Financial Post Magazine* described prostitution as a billion-dollar business in Canada, but reported that the money is spread out among thousands of people working coast to coast. Criminal organizations can make more money running bingo halls than escort services, and they could do it with less effort.

Still, there are always exceptions. I have never seen an Asian woman working a stroll in Toronto and I've seen very few ads placed in the entertainment tabloids by Asian call-girls. I have been told by experienced customers that the bulk of Asian prostitution in Toronto occurs in brothels controlled by Asian gangs. The women are not in these houses by choice. They keep very little of the money they earn, and they have no freedom. Some aren't even in the country legally. This isn't prostitution, it's sexual slavery.

Even organizations which posed no overt threat to the brothels in Toronto's Asian communities — advocacy groups such as Maggie's and CORP — were unable to penetrate the barriers and meet the women. In a secretive environment such as this mobsters can flourish and the more you criminalize an activity, the more you make it the exclusive realm of the criminal. It's difficult for gangsters to seize control of an activity that operates legally and overtly. Another reason for decriminalizing prostitution.

The antagonistic relationship between prostitutes and the police is not working to anyone's benefit. Cops can't control prostitution and pros feel they aren't being served or protected by the police. Police critics claim the relationship between the cops and the community as a whole is poor and that police forces exist mainly to serve and protect their own interests. At the end of eighties a new-old concept of policing arose which critics and coppers alike heralded as the way of the future — community policing.

Sir Robert Peel best described the concept when he said, "The police are the public and the public are the police." In a June 1996 fact sheet, the department of the Solicitor General of Canada said community policing allows the people and the community to play a key role in deciding how they will be policed. "It is about people and partnerships — it's policing *for* communities rather than *of* communities. It brings police closer to the communities they serve, and allows the police to play an active role in dealing with crime. It is also about the police and the community working together to solve and prevent local crime problems. What is important about community policing is that it allows for a range of policing strategies and problem-solving tactics which can be tailored to the communities they serve."

People and partnerships, new strategies, problem solving; if this all sounds too good to be true for prostitutes it's because it is. Edmonton's police force set up a prototype community policing project in 1990. Known as the Neighbourhood Foot Patrol Project, it became a community policing model for many police departments across Canada. Constable Rick Saunders, a cop who walked the beat in the downtown neighbourhood of McCauley, was a member of this patrol. McCauley was a stroll and residents complained to Saunders about the high volume of traffic in the neighbourhood, the syringes and condoms found on private property, and the men who propositioned women on the street. He began talking with property owners and later, by speaking at community meetings, he convinced homeowners that they could do something about the street prostitution in McCauley. He eventually organized a public anti-prostitution protest and invited the media. The targets of the protest were the customers of prostitutes, and it received a lot of attention from the press. For a short time the number of cars cruising through McCauley declined and Constable Saunders claimed a small victory.

However, business soon resumed, and Saunders organized a second protest in the fall of 1990 to coincide with a mayoralty election campaign. This protest attracted plenty of media, as well as numerous community leaders who showed up with prepared statements and rehearsed responses. Organizers made sure that there were extra placards available for any candidates and their hangers-on who happened by. No one who could benefit from the event missed it, but it didn't drive prostitution out of McCauley. Community anti-prostitution activism increased in anticipation of the hookers moving on and other protests were held in adjoining neighbourhoods, with the full cooperation of the Edmonton Police Services. The police service went so far as to declare 1992 as the Year of the John, and concentrated on charging clients as well as prostitutes. The effects of these efforts were later summed up by the Edmonton Police Service in their own report, *New Directions.* "None of these initiatives have made a long-term impact on Edmonton's problem of prostitution. In most cases, prostitutes moved to other areas of the city. No 'ivory tower' solution will cure prostitution."

Although the Edmonton police described its actions in McCauley as innovative, they're old hat to anyone familiar with anti-prostitution activism in Toronto. There the police supported the property owners and went so far as to encourage them to actively protest street prostitution. So long as community police encourage or support NIMBY reactions to street prostitution, the working women will have no reason to trust the police. For the whores, no matter how much things change, they continue to remain the same.

chapter 6

Living On
the Avails

The language of prostitution includes powerful words such as "whore," "john," "bordello," and each one conjures up its own set of images and emotions. But no single word associated with prostitution invokes darker images or more heartfelt emotions than does "pimp," *the* word which, for many, sums up everything that is wrong with this ancient profession. In simple legal terms a pimp is someone who lives off the earnings of a prostitute. Such a broad definition can include many people most of us don't think of when we hear that word. Children live off the earnings of prostitute mothers; husbands, lovers, siblings, perhaps even parents, can all meet the basic requirements for being classified as pimps by the courts.

Kathleen Barry, the American founder of The Coalition Against Trafficking in Women, prefers an even broader definition. She says that anyone who promotes the sexual exploitation and commodification of women is a pimp. Barry considers all prostitution to be exploitive, regardless of how or why individual prostitutes enter the trade. Anyone who is in any way involved in a personal relationship with a prostitute but does not try to get the whore out of the Business is, according to Barry, a pimp. Acceptance of the work is unacceptable to her. For me a pimp has always been someone who uses violence or other means to force a prostitute to work for him and who may also use psychological abuse to convince the prostitute to stay with him and hand over her money. A pimp may have more than one woman working for him, but based on what other prostitutes, both indoor and outdoor, have told me, most pimps only run one or two women; the large stable seems to be more a creation of Hollywood than of Canadian streets.

In many respects a pimp–prostitute relationship is similar to any other kind of abusive relationship. A bond — a "good" bond — is established early on between the abuser and the victim. Pimps may first offer a woman who is not a prostitute flattery, shelter, clothing, drugs or affection. Then he starts applying the pressure. The pimp may ask the woman to "just do this one little favour for me," or he may insist on being repaid for the kindness he's shown her. The woman has no money, so the pimp tells her how to go out and make it. If the woman is intrigued by the idea of prostitution, he may simply encourage her to get to work — for him. Either way she is expected to turn over some, or all, of her earnings to the pimp. If the woman complies, fine; if she doesn't, she's punished. Women have been beaten, whipped with coat hangers, burnt with cigarettes and curling irons, shot with stun guns — the litany of horrors is long and varied. Or, instead of using violence (damaged merchandise doesn't fetch a good price in the market), the pimp may withhold something the woman wants or needs in order to entice her to continue working for him — drugs if she's an addict, money, love — or he may threaten her, "Work for me or I'll kill you." All of these techniques are used by abusive partners in traditional relationships, they're not exclusive to prostitute–pimp relationships.

Considering the abuse, threats and violence, why do the pros stay with their pimps? Many don't, they just pack up and leave. Fear of retaliation is one reason why many women stay, but not the only one. Pimps offer the women whom they have convinced to become prostitutes two things they are led to believe they cannot get anywhere else — protection and understanding. Pimps are purveyors of illusions. The protection offered is usually protection from other pimps or from aggressive women on the street, and is rarely there when it's needed. The understanding is a little different. Many prostitutes get absolutely no acceptance outside of the sex trade. The police and the courts call them criminals, homeowners and residents groups call them scourges, circle jerks call them everything under the sun, many customers look down their noses at the women they hire. In the midst of all this a pimp can offer acceptance, even love, and no one should be surprised when the women respond accordingly. The acceptance and the love may not be real, but the illusory affection the prostitutes receive is better than the very real hatred they feel on the street.

While the most ardent of the anti-prostitution advocates insist that more than ninety per cent of prostitution is controlled by pimps, an increasing number of prostitutes are challenging this claim. Pros say roughly twenty per cent of the women currently working in the Biz in Canada are involved with pimps and this figure includes the experienced prostitutes who have purposefully chosen their men. When a prostitute chooses, she enters into a financial arrangement with a man (or a woman, if the pro prefers); she gives him a percentage of her earnings, and he is expected to be there for her. The arrangement ends when the participants decide to break it up. In some respects this arrangement is similar to the traditional pimp–prostitute relationship; the man is expected to provide understanding and acceptance that the woman cannot find outside the Business. Abusive pimps don't come through, but chosen men, according to the women involved, do. Men who are chosen know that if they want the money to keep coming in, they have to keep up their end of the bargain. Sometimes they are sex partners of the pros, but not always: it's first and foremost a financial agreement, not an emotional commitment.

People who condemn prostitution dismiss the claim that some prostitutes willingly engage in choosing. They argue that these women are so brainwashed they only believe they have chosen, and that the relationship is by nature abusive. Prostitution is so misunderstood because whenever working women speak up and say things about the Business which contradict generally held beliefs, or challenge the prostitute-equals-victim equation, the comments are disbelieved or ignored. Instead, words spoken by people who have never turned a trick in their lives are taken as gospel. I've never worked for a pimp. I've never appeared helpless or otherwise susceptible to a pimp so I've never been approached by one. David, the man who passed my phone number and description around to his friends during my first year in prostitution, was not a pimp. I did not give him any of my money and he never abused me in any way.

I had never heard of choosing and the first time I did I didn't believe what I was told. My attitude changed after the process was explained to me by four different women over a period of a few months. The ritual of choosing is not all that shocking when you think about it. Women and men have been entering into arrangements of convenience for thousands of years and today when straight people choose to pay someone to provide acceptance or understanding we call it going to a therapist.

Prostitutes want the right to associate with and give their money to whomever they see fit, but in Canada it's illegal for anyone to live off the earnings of a prostitute or to be habitually in the company of one. It's also illegal for anyone to procure anyone else for the purpose of prostitution. These rulings make up the essence of our anti-pimping laws and Canadian activists want these laws abolished because, they argue, the laws criminalize all people who have relationships with prostitutes. One of the basic tenets of our criminal justice system is that the accused is innocent until proven guilty. Not so if someone is charged with habitually being in the company of a prostitute. The accused must prove he or she does not live off the prostitute's earnings in order to avoid being found guilty of living on the avails — pimping. It's easy to see why prostitutes oppose the anti-pimping laws. Husbands, lovers, friends and children are all regularly in the company of prostitutes, so technically they can all be charged and convicted of pimping, unless they prove otherwise. The way our anti-pimping laws are written, it can be difficult for an unemployed husband or boyfriend to prove that he isn't living off the earnings of a pro when she is paying the rent and putting food on the table.

My partner, Karen, never forced me to give her any of the money I earned working as a prostitute, but I often did. I bought her gifts, paid the bills, even gave her cash (hard evidence of a pimping offence, if the currency was marked). At one point, when Karen was between jobs, she lived completely on the avails of prostitution. She was knowingly and actively breaking another subsection of Section 212 of the Criminal Code (the anti-pimping law). In fact she broke a couple of these subsections (Section 212 has thirteen parts). She lived with and was habitually in the company of a prostitute (me) and she was habitually in the company of other prostitutes (my friends). On top of all this, she could often be found in a brothel (the home of one of my friends, which doubled as a workplace). Theoretically any combination of these offences could have earned Karen up to ten years in prison. Yet Karen hardly fits the "scum-of-the-earth" profile of the typical pimp. Nor do I, though I had briefly pimped a woman in Sault Ste. Marie in the mid-eighties (more about this in Chapter 7).

Advocates of tough anti-pimping legislation claim the laws are necessary to protect prostitutes from abusive, exploitive men, yet we find abusive men living off the earnings of women working in all kinds of occupations. What do we call wife-beaters who live off the earnings of teachers or waitresses? We don't call them pimps and our lawmakers have not written specific legislation to protect women in these occupations either. Why do prostitutes warrant special treatment? Many working women have said it's because society sees whores as being so contemptible that it's going to punish anyone who has the gall to enter into relationships with them. There doesn't seem to be any other reasonable explanation for the existence of the anti-pimping laws, so the prostitutes' claims must be taken seriously. If the anti-pimping laws were done away with, violent pimps could be prosecuted and punished under the same laws that protect all other women, regardless of occupation, from abuse and exploitation. Prostitutes would also receive more real protection. When a prostitute calls the police and says her pimp is beating her, the cops say they will investigate the matter. They also tell the pro it will be up to her to lay charges against her attacker. When a non-prostitute woman calls the police and says her husband is beating her, the cops show up five minutes later, kick down the door and arrest and charge the man. The removal of these laws would also remove the stigma attached to the legitimate partners of prostitutes, which in turn would make prostitutes a little more equal to all other Canadian women — but maybe not everyone wants to see that happen.

Morris Glasgow of North Preston, Nova Scotia, and Sheila Devlin of New York City were both pimps in the eyes of the police and the courts, yet the two were treated very differently. Glasgow was young, black and violent. He attacked a fifteen-year-old and a seventeen-year-old girl with a stun gun and had the reputation of being a kingpin of prostitution in Halifax. Devlin was young, white and well-heeled. She ran a New York escort service which was reputed to cater to the wealthy if not the powerful. Glasgow's women were experienced prostitutes. Devlin refused to hire experienced pros for her agency, preferring only pretty young women in their early twenties who had never worked in the sex trade. She frowned on the idea of her escorts carrying condoms and told the women not to use them unless the customers insisted. Both Glasgow and Devlin were eventually charged and convicted of prostitution-related offences. At the time of her arrest, it was discovered that Sheila Devlin was the alias of Sydney Biddle Barrows, who could trace her lineage back to the Mayflower. She was subsequently dubbed the Mayflower Madam by the U.S. media.

Morris Glasgow was sentenced to seven years in prison for assault, weapons charges and living on the avails of prostitution. Barrows was convicted of promoting prostitution and fined five thousand dollars. Both pimps showed little regard for the women in their employ; Glasgow was violent and Barrows was dangerous, or at the very least naïve and stupid. The New York City madam was not violent, like Glasgow, but she probably put far more women in danger. She told her whores to jump up and down in the bathroom after having sex with their tricks, a silly and possibly deadly substitute for condom use in the age of AIDS. She felt her clients were less likely to be infected with sexually transmitted diseases because they were straight and willing to pay two hundred dollars for an hour of an escort's time. Barrows' hookers, unfamiliar with the realities of prostitution, and perhaps even with sex, likely believed this myth and followed their madam's instructions. Neither sexual orientation nor money has ever protected anyone from disease. Following her conviction Barrows wrote a book about her experiences as a madam and went on numerous speaking tours during which she told curious, mainly female, audiences how to keep their men at home and happy.

*   *   *

Young people flock to cities like Toronto looking for a better, more prosperous, or more exciting life, but too many end up on the street where poverty is the common denominator and survival the prime motivator. To a teenager who has been sleeping in a park or over a subway grill an offer of a decent meal, new clothes, a place to stay and maybe even recreational substances can be very seductive.

Pimps have a reputation for turning children into prostitutes. I've read many newspaper stories about prostitutes who said they were forced to start turning tricks when they were in their early teens, or even younger. I've spoken with adult prostitutes who say they began working when they were children. Yet I have never met a juvenile prostitute, not even during the time I was doing AIDS outreach and spending hours on the streets, night after night, talking with street hookers about AIDS prevention. Young people — street youth — were given the highest priority when I was doing AIDS work. Later, as a journalist researching stories on prostitution, I interviewed the staff of a social service organization which worked with Toronto's street prostitutes. They acknowledged the existence of juvenile prostitution but insisted it was rare, and many of their staff said they had never met any child prostitutes. My partner, Karen, who has spent the last five years working in women's social services in Toronto, has met and spoken with only one juvenile prostitute.

Many studies state that a high percentage (often eighty to ninety per cent) of prostitute women began working when they were in their early teens. Women constantly drift in and out of the Business; new faces regularly appear on the strolls and new ads appear in the back pages of entertainment tabloids. If it is true that the majority of prostitutes, particularly street prostitutes, begin hooking when they are very young, where are the all the young prostitutes? In a city the size of Toronto, which has more than a half-dozen strolls, you would think that baby-faced hookers would be a common sight, but they're not. I know that juvenile prostitution exists, but I believe it's less common than the media would have us believe.

For the last ten to fifteen years Toronto's prostitute population has varied between 3,500 and 5,000 women and men. The majority are women who work indoors. (These figures are based on estimates arrived at by the Metro Police and the Canadian Organization for the Rights of Prostitutes.). Street prostitution accounts for roughly ten to twenty per cent of these totals, depending on the time of year, so on any given night you should find a minimum of 350 to 500 prostitutes working the city's strolls. In June 1996, the police said there were 300 prostitutes, sixteen years old or younger, working in Toronto. Between January and June of that year the police pulled twenty — TWENTY! — under-age hookers off the street. They were turned over to the Children's Aid Society, which encouraged them to go home.

During the same six-month period the police busted fifty pimps — six were convicted. These figures are very disturbing. Priscilla Alexander, at one time the co-director of the U.S. prostitutes' rights organization COYOTE and the executive director of the U.S. National Task Force on Prostitution, estimates that juvenile prostitutes see an average of 300 customers a year (in comparison an adult streetwalker will see about 1,500 customers a year). If indeed there are 300 under-age pros working in Toronto, juvenile prostitution accounted for about 90,000 cases of juvenile sexual abuse that went unreported in the city in 1996 and the police efforts to curb this problem are pathetic. But I also wonder if the police estimate of the extent of juvenile prostitution in Toronto is accurate. Most of these young prostitutes likely worked the streets, but if even one-third of them worked indoors, that left 200 teen hookers working outside, in plain view of the police and social service agencies. Where are these prostitutes and what's happening to them?

In the spring of 1996 Metro Councillor Brian Ashton called Toronto the "runaway capital of Canada." Many young people, particularly girls and young women, have turned tricks in order to survive in the harsh environment of our city's streets but this is survival sex, not prostitution. A prostitute is someone who has made it her job to sell sex. There's a huge difference between seeing clients night after night because that's what you do to earn a living and turning the odd trick in order to buy some real food, or to afford a room in a decent hotel so you can get a full night's sleep. Prostitutes' rights activists, including Valerie Scott of CORP, have criticized youth service agencies for saying that kids who engage in survival sex are prostitutes. Now more agencies which deal with street youth are acknowledging the differences between survival sex and prostitution and they are looking at ways of offering young people alternatives to both. Law enforcement is not the answer. Locking up pimps will only open up turfs to new pimps, and in any case, juvenile prostitution, as well as survival sex, will occur in their absence. Customer crack-downs only deprive young prostitutes of income, leaving them worse off than before. Solutions to juvenile prostitution must be found elsewhere, and simply sending young people home is no solution. If a child runs away to escape sexual or emotional abuse or violence, our city streets, as mean as they are, may be safer or at least feel more comfortable than the family home.

Most of the prostitutes I've known have never been involved in abusive pimp-pro relationships but all of them have, or had, the kind of relationships where the other persons could have been charged with pimping offences. While I was with Maggie's, many pros told me their boyfriends and lovers were busted for pimping even though there was no coercion or abuse in the relationships. "My boyfriend was convicted because he had no job," said one woman. "The judge said to my boyfriend, 'You haven't got a job so you must be living off of her and that makes you a pimp.' Now he's sitting in jail, just because he hasn't got a job." Non-prostitutes (and some former pros) insist that working women need to be protected from predatory pimps masquerading as lover material. These guardians forget that there are other laws in the Criminal Code which can do that.

If you polled the general public and asked, "Who is most likely to be violent with a prostitute?" pimps would probably get the nod, with customers coming in second. When I spoke with prostitutes about violence, I got a different response. Rogue cops led the pack of those who inflict violence on working women, followed by vigilante groups, rowdies and circle jerks. Customers and pimps weren't in the running for top honours, but suffering through an act of violence can permanently change your view of the world — when it happened to me, my views on prostitution changed dramatically.

In the late eighties I managed Jean's Escort Service in Sault Ste. Marie. I also turned a few tricks on the side whenever a customer asked about specialty services — the kind I had provided when I worked in Toronto. One night, a man staying at the Holiday Inn booked me over the phone. He said he was into bondage and domination, but nothing too heavy. I met the fellow, a tall, fit-looking dark-haired man in his early forties, in his hotel room. He seemed fine, but my sixth sense told me something wasn't right. Normally I would have made up some excuse and walked away but because I couldn't figure out what was bothering me, I ignored my internal warnings. The client had a touch of liquor on his breath but he wasn't visibly drunk and he didn't sound drunk as we exchanged pleasantries and small talk. He gave me my money, then invited me to use his bathroom to get ready. There on the sink was a small shaving mirror which looked as though it had been dusted with a fine white powder. I tasted the powder and realized that my date was stoned on cocaine. Foolishly, I thought I could handle the situation.

When I came out of the bathroom the man was on the bed. As I began shimmying out of my underwear, he kicked me square in the jaw, hard. My head snapped back, the rest of me followed, and I collapsed as if I had been shot. He then sprung up and lunged at me but I rolled out of his way. As he went for a knife on the bedside table, I bolted out the door, naked, into the hallway.

When my attacker chased me, I shouted, "Hey buddy, you're naked you know," and he stopped dead in his tracks. I turned and faced him. He dropped the knife and stood there looking confused. Suddenly a change came over him. He apologized and begged me to go back into the room.

I insisted that he first kick the knife out to me. Then I told him to get my stuff — my clothes, my trick bag, the money, everything — and throw it all out to me. He did as I asked, and, while he gathered up my belongings, I picked up the knife, which turned out to be a letter opener, and threw it down the hallway. Once I had my clothes, I dressed in a flash, stuffed everything else into my bag and began walking.

"Wait a minute," he called, "you said you'd come back. You promised."

"Call your lawyer," I shouted over my shoulder as I began running towards the stairs. I didn't stop moving until I was out of the hotel and in a cab heading home.

I gave myself the once-over in my bathroom mirror. His kick had cracked one of my teeth and loosened a couple of its neighbours. My gums were bleeding and the front of my blouse was spattered red. I started chugging shots of whisky as I cleaned myself up and wrestled with the idea of going to the cops. Physically I wasn't in bad shape but emotionally I was a mess and my drinking didn't help. Eventually anger took over and I threw on some fresh clothes and made my way to the Sault's police station. I fantasized about charging my bad date with attempted murder but I would have had better luck getting him charged with double-parking. When I told my story to the cops on duty, they did everything but burst out laughing and I'm sure they did after I left. They just couldn't imagine someone who looked like a six-foot,

160-pound man turning tricks in their town, let alone
getting attacked by a drugged-up customer. I knew I didn't
have a hope of convincing the cops to make a move on my
bad date so I went home dejected, finished off the bottle of
whisky, and passed out in bed. I spent most of the next day
feeling sorry for myself.

These days the cops and the courts are doing a better job
of responding to violence against prostitutes, but there is still
a belief that they somehow deserve the beatings, rapes and
robberies they suffer. I've witnessed this attitude many times
over the years as I've participated in community meetings
and watched and listened to audiences responding to prostitutes speaking out about violence. There are those who feel
prostitutes are just bad girls, and when you don't like the
victims, it's easy to blame them for the nasty things that
happen to them. Then there are those who say they have
nothing against the women but they do have a problem with
the work. "Well … if the girls were doing something else,
those horrible things wouldn't happen to them." Horrible
things happen to people regardless of what they do for a
living. The same year that I was attacked, a friend of mine
was robbed at gunpoint while working in a Sault Ste. Marie
convenience store. Prostitutes cannot be considered targets
of opportunity for violent offenders and an assault on a
prostitute must be treated the same way as an assault on
anyone else.

Protection is the reason most often used for justifying all
of our prostitution laws, not just the anti-pimping law. Prostitutes must be protected from pimps and rough customers;
non-prostitute women must be protected from men cruising
for sex; men must be protected from temptation and sexually

transmitted diseases; neighbourhoods must be protected from an influx of prostitutes; politicians must be protected from angry ratepayer groups; children must be protected from everything; and everybody must be protected from everybody else — including themselves. None of these laws protected me from my attacker in the Holiday Inn, nor do they protect the many prostitutes who experience some form of work-related violence during their careers. If anything, the laws may protect the very villains they are supposed to threaten. If a woman decides to take legal action against a pimp, she knows that, among other things, she'll have to come out as a prostitute (with all the risks that entails) and to some her occupation will make her an unreliable witness. Even in a courtroom where justice is supposed to be meted out fairly, a prostitute's word may be undermined by prejudice.

chapter 7

Northern
Exposure

Sault Ste. Marie, Ontario, is known for its locks on the Saint Mary's River, a railroad tour of the picturesque Agawa Canyon, and for being across the border from Sneaky Pete's, the best-known whorehouse in Soo, Michigan. Pete's was known to just about every taxi driver, dispatcher and cop in the two cities, and probably every man who grew up in either the American or the Canadian Sault. Pete's wasn't a classy bordello by any stretch of the imagination. Its popularity wasn't based on the availability of beautiful women, its skilled sexual artisans, or even cheap liquor; it was popular because it was the only game in town. There was no piano player, no crystal chandeliers, no exotic play rooms — just women, beds and someone to collect the money. Sault, Ontario, had nothing comparable, so half the brothel's customers were Canadians, and Pete's took Canadian money at par.

I moved to the Sault in the fall of 1979. The retail skills I had learned while working in Sudbury paid off when Leisure World, a Toronto-based chain of hobby shops, offered me a job managing its Sault Ste. Marie store. I took the job and soon was working fifty to sixty hours a week, and although I enjoyed the work, I felt I was making more money for Leisure World's shareholders than for me. I put in an offer to buy the store and entered into negotiations but nothing came of them. I was determined to own my own shop and with the help of family and friends I scraped together enough money to go into business for myself in the summer of 1983. As a store owner I worked even longer hours and made less money than I did as a manager. Although my little hobby shop was moderately successful, after one year I gave it all up. I sold the fixtures and merchandise, paid off my debts and tried to figure out what I wanted to do next. In the meantime, I drove a cab. Cab driving and prostitution have something in common — you have to hustle to make money.

During my three years as a Leisure World manager I made over twenty trips to Toronto to attend trade fairs, business meetings, and to purchase goods for the store. While on these trips, I worked the city's bars. In recent years escort services and pagers have killed bar prostitution in larger cities like Toronto. Men looking to hire hookers don't have to hang around singles bars wondering whether the lone woman they see is working or just out alone; all they have to do is pick up a phone. In the early eighties, however, bar prostitution was pretty common and could be profitable provided the prostitutes weren't too obvious about what they were doing and were careful not to get drunk. A number of Toronto's downtown hotels were famous for their working bars. The Royal York was perhaps the best known of these — one old saying claimed, "no one has to sleep alone at the Royal" — but there were many others. The Chelsea had a bar called The Chelsea Bun which was a haven for Frank Sinatra sound-alikes, other assorted lounge lizards, and hookers. Even I pulled dates out of the Bun and I only dabbled in cocktail hooking.

Bar hooking works much the same as street prostitution but the weather is more consistent, and you can sit down. I'd go into a bar or tavern in the early evening, order a light drink and nurse it until some guy showed an interest in me. Initial contact was made by eye, followed by the friendly smile. Sometimes interested men would send drinks to my table then trail them to the seat beside me; usually they just walked right over. I never bothered small-talking the men first, but made things clear right away. A few guys were offended because I wouldn't sleep with them for free, some just walked away. The tricks slipped me their money and off we went. I was fussy about who I picked up and ignored come-ons from rough looking or drunk men. Most bartenders and wait staff were cool about what I did and didn't bother me. The worst that could happen was being asked to leave and told never to come back, but in the bar scene nobody gets barred from anywhere forever.

*   *   *

I made a number of friends in the Sault but few were closer than Carol. Carol wanted to attend the Sault's Algoma University but couldn't afford to. She wanted a job so she could earn the money for tuition but there were no opportunities for a woman who lacked both skills and experience. She was trapped on the no-money, no-experience, no-skill, no-job treadmill. Carol lived on welfare and was deeply frustrated by her apparently hopeless lot in life. Carol's parents were in no position to help her, financially or otherwise.

When Carol and I became friends it wasn't long before I began to tell her about my experiences in the Business. She was intrigued by my stories and suddenly announced one day that she had decided to become a prostitute. Here was a job for which she was qualified — she had the skills and experience was not necessary. But there were problems. There was no neighbourhood stroll. She also didn't want to go public, which meant that working the Sault's bars was out of the question, as was advertising her services as a freelance call-girl. (She was afraid that people would recognize her phone number.) Furthermore she wasn't interested in Sneaky Pete's: wanted to work in Canada.

Carol needed a pimp and turned to me. "You're perfect, Alex. We trust each other, you know the Biz, and you drive taxi so you meet guys all the time who are looking for women just like me." Carol was a bright woman, tall, buxom, with auburn hair that flowed loosely around her shoulders. She wasn't model-thin but more luscious, more hedonistic looking — imagine a heavy-metal milk maid. She was well read, opinionated and very outgoing. My instincts told me that some of her customers would find her intimidating but others would fall head-over-heels in love with her.

Television newsreaders often use expressions like "the places where men go looking for sex" when covering stories on prostitution, but in my experience, men look for sex everywhere. While driving cab, I picked up all sorts of guys in search of sex. Once Carol and I worked out the particulars, I took a number of these men to her. Our business arrangement was very simple — she charged her dates $150 and I got twenty per cent. She told me when she wanted to work and for how long. There was no coercion, no extortion. We were friends who had an arrangement, and it was a profitable one.

I delivered men to Carol's doorstep for almost two years while she went to school. Most of Carol's friends were friends of mine and knew about our arrangement, but a few accused me of taking advantage of her situation and forcing her into prostitution. I felt odd about taking customers to Carol, because I, like many of our friends, thought pimps were evil. But Carol constantly reminded me that I was doing something she wanted me to do, and she said, "If you don't do this for me I'll find someone else who will." And so we continued until she moved to Sudbury in order to further her studies. There she picked up a good part-time job and was able to leave the sex trade. She did well in Sudbury, both academically and personally, and the last I heard she was working in her chosen field and involved with someone very special to her.

Compared to Toronto, Sault Ste. Marie was an inexpensive city to live in. From the money I earned as a cabbie and as Carol's ersatz pimp, I saved enough money for a holiday. Toronto, with its relatively wide-open sex industry, still drew me like a magnet so I drove down and stayed with my sister, Tanya. During the days we hung out together; in the evenings — unbeknownst to her — I went out and worked the bars. I didn't care whether I broke, I just wanted to feel like I was part of the Business. Hooking gave me glimpses of a different world, the underworld, which seemed to me more colourful, more intense, and while harder, lived with greater enthusiasm than much of the straight world was. It also introduced me to people like Stanley, who in turn introduced me to Dorothy, who changed my life.

I picked up Stanley while working a gay bar. He was a senior citizen. You could say he had one foot in the grave, but he dragged himself around with the other one faster, and with more enthusiasm, than many twenty-year-olds. Stanley had spent his adult life working for a large company and by the time he retired he had earned both the gold watch and a good retirement package. His wife was dead and his kids were grown — he was a free man. Sexual orientation meant nothing to him — he'd sleep with anyone he found attractive and who would have him. Most were prostitutes. He and I got along from word go. He took me for a pro the moment he laid eyes on me and his first words to me were: "How much will it cost to have you run around with me all night?" His directness bowled me over and I blurted out "Five hundred dollars." "Fine," he said, "here's half," as he tossed a wad of bills onto my table.

As we walked out onto the street I caught our reflections in a glass storefront. I towered over the old man. "We're an odd-looking couple," Stan commented, noticing where my eyes were focused, "but don't worry about it. Compared to some of the people you're going to meet we're positively normal looking. He took me to one after-hours club after another, their themes changing like street lights. In one place he stopped to talk to a friend while a room packed full of leather-clad men hopped and bopped to some dance tune. Next we dropped into a very straight, very conservative place where all the men and women looked like bank tellers or real-estate agents.

Stanley didn't strike me as the board-room type. "Why are we here?" I asked.

"We're looking for a friend of mine, someone I want you to meet."

Our search took us to a trendy hair salon where a party raged. "I don't expect to find her here," my guide shouted over the din of loud music and screaming conversations, "but friends of hers are here and they may know what she's up to." Stanley darted away and I lost him in the crowd. The party-goers were all grotesquely beautiful. Half-naked men dressed in leather, lace or denim danced with each other or no one in particular. Women flaunted miles of cleavage and stockinged leg. Black was the predominant colour — black clothes, black walls, black light which gave pale flesh a blueish lumi-nescence. Suddenly Stanley emerged from the crowd. "She's not here and no one knows where she is. Let's go."

It had begun to rain and the street resembled a long strip of black ice. "Are you game for one more place before calling it a night?" challenged Stanley. I nodded. We went to a nearby all-night coffee shop where we talked until the dawn. Stan didn't discuss sex, something I thought would come up sooner or later. Nor did he discuss the mysterious friend he wanted me to meet. We agreed to spend the next night together and he assured me that our search would end. I left him in the coffee shop and caught a cab to Tanya's.

The next day, Stanley looked fresh and rested. We started with a simple supper in a small restaurant he liked, during which we took care of the financial end of the business. He gave me another five hundred dollars and his home phone number, "just in case you should ever need it." We passed on dessert and took a cab to one of the many older buildings that were scattered around Toronto's downtown. We went in a side door and down a narrow flight of stairs. The dimly lit stairwell led to a large, low-ceilinged room that reminded me of the big rec rooms in suburban homes. Tables and chairs were located haphazardly throughout; a couple of people milled about carrying trays of drinks, others sat at tables chatting, reading newspapers or swirling olives in triangular glasses. The room was lit with small lamps which turned each table into an island of orange light. Soft music filled holes in the background. Stanley led me to one of the islands at which sat an older, bespectacled woman dressed in a plainly cut, flower-print dress. Her light brown hair was streaked with grey and she wore little make-up. She smiled at us as Stanley rushed to her side and kissed her on the cheek. I shook her hand as Stanley introduced us, then he and I sat down. This was Dorothy.

Dorothy owned a flower shop in Hamilton but spent as much time in Toronto, her home town, as she could. She drifted in and out of the club scene "but look at me," she laughed, "I don't exactly fit in, do I?" Recalling the animated zombies I had watched the night before, I wondered why anyone would *want* to fit in. Stanley excused himself and went chasing off after an imaginary friend. We chatted about him for a few minutes until Dorothy asked, "You aren't comfortable trying to be a man, are you?"

"No," I said, *sotto voce*, "I never have been."

"Neither was I," she said, her eyes flashing through her glasses. "And we don't have to whisper here. I know this place. No one minds and no one will bother you."

The slight peculiarities I had noticed about Dorothy now made sense — her large hands and firm, confident grip, her deep voice. "Souvenirs of another life," she explained. "Stan wanted us to meet because he saw in you the same things he saw in me eons ago. We've been friends forever and he stood by me every step of the way. As I watched you walk over to my table and saw how you conduct yourself, I thought 'Stan's right, she's no guy.'"

I nodded in quiet agreement. Dorothy ordered drinks. In less than half an hour tears rolled down my face, as layers of confusion, misunderstanding, fear and loathing were delicately peeled away, one by one. The waiters hovered periodically to make sure everything was all right and Dorothy reassured them that everything was, indeed, all right. I learned more about myself that evening than I had learned during my entire life. Our conversation was emotionally exhausting but exhilirating. Dorothy taught me that I was the expert on myself and, apart from a few particulars, when I would need outside help, all the answers were inside me. I have no idea exactly how long we sat in that little pub talking; it was dark when I went in and dark when Dorothy and I came out. She stood next to me on the sidewalk and held one of my large hands in hers. "People make a fuss over hands you know, feet too. You'll come to hate one or the other of your own. You'll think they're too big, not dainty enough, not ladylike. Don't get too worked up over them. Your hands, your feet, all your parts are the size they are because of your height, not your gender. You're a big girl and you will just have to get used to it."

She told me to call her if I was ever in Hamilton. "Stanley has my number — oh, before I forget, call him tomorrow. He's very curious about how our little chat went. Pretty well, I'd say."

"Very well," I agreed.

She caught the first cab that came along and sped off to wherever she was staying. I walked a ways before hailing my own cab. The evening with Dorothy had made me a changed person, and the cabbie's standard question, "Where to, sir," seemed more inappropriate than ever.

My holiday time finally ran out and I had to go back up north. As I drove the seven hours back to the Sault, I kept rethinking the long conversation I had had with Dorothy and tried to figure out what to do next. I bought half a dozen books on transsexualism, thinking all I needed in order to make decisions was information. Dorothy had told me so much, but she could only give me one woman's point of view; I wanted more. Once home I devoured the books. The personal anecdotes of women who had gone through the whole experience were the most informative, and the similarities between their stories and my own were striking and more than a little frightening. By reading these stories I learned that if I was going to deal with my condition by seeking sex reassignment surgery, I would have to overcome numerous barriers built up by psychiatrists and doctors. I couldn't even imagine what that would be like. I also knew I had to get back down to Toronto, and that proved to be my first hurdle. I didn't have enough money saved to afford a permanent move. I was getting fed up with the taxi business. My fellow drivers and I worked long hours for what were often pitiful wages and, because we weren't organized, we had no say in our working conditions. I saw myself trapped in the Sault for years.

I was wondering whether I could make a living hooking in the Sault when I came across an ad in the *Sault Star* for a manager for Jean's Escort Service. The ad surprised me, not because someone was opening an escort service in the Sault but that no one had done it sooner. The city struck me as an ideal place to open a service but I had lived in the Sault for seven years and hadn't heard anything about an escort service until now. Prostitution goes on in smaller cities but is conducted differently than in a city like Toronto. Sudbury and Sault Ste. Marie don't have strolls, for instance; the only small city that I have ever visited that had a stroll was Thunder Bay. My partner, Karen, grew up in the Bay and she explains that because of the city's isolation people living there create their own versions of features and services found in larger cities. If a Sudburian wants to cruise a stroll, he can drive to Toronto. Men from the Sault looking for street prostitutes can go to Detroit. Thunder Bay has no close large urban neighbour, so a stroll developed on Simpson Street after the police closed down most of the city's brothels. Bar prostitution goes on in all of these smaller cities. In Sudbury hookers can usually be found in the Ledo or the Prospect hotel lounges every weekend. In the Sault hookers pull dates out of the Eastgate lounge. But not every potential customer likes going to bars to find whores; it can be confusing and embarrassing for someone not in the know. Brothels offer a viable alternative but brothels in smaller centres can have their own problems. Once a house opens for business, everybody learns about the place, either through visits or rumours.

I figured an escort service in the Sault could not help but be successful and when I met Alfred — Alf — the owner of

Jean's, I told him so. Alf wasn't some smooth-talking, sharp-dressing dude from Detroit; he was a retired Canadian steel worker who had too much time on his hands and just enough money to play around a bit. Alf was short, fat, gruff and wore work boots because he worked, not because he wanted to make a fashion statement. He drank, chain-smoked, would never ask for sun-dried tomatoes on his pizza and couldn't care less if he was "politically correct." Depending on your point of view, he was either the salt of the earth or some kind of hick. Since Alf knew very little about prostitution, he needed someone who could hire and fire the women, work the phones, and make sure everybody stayed out of jail. All he knew about prostitution was what his current girlfriend, Rita, who pulled dates out of the Central Tavern between welfare cheques, told him — and that, I soon realized, was next to nothing.

Alf hired me during our first meeting. He had a few women ready to work, including Rita. I met with them the next day to lay out the ground rules. The women set their own hours and days of work but everybody had to be available at least five days a week. The service screened all the calls and set up all the dates. I said I would try to see that everybody got approximately the same amount of business but I couldn't make any promises. The service got one-third of the agreed-upon price of a date, the women kept their tips. We weren't a whorehouse, so no one could bring customers to the office. Alf drove the women to and from their calls. No one could get drunk or high while working and no one could bring drugs into the office. If anyone had any kind of trouble with a customer, she was to call me immediately so we could get her out. I figured these simple rules would keep everybody honest and the cops off our backs. The women agreed.

Alf said he would pay me a couple of hundred dollars a week until things got rolling, then I would receive a bonus of twenty-five dollars for every date I arranged. I hoped that under this arrangement I could save enough money to leave the Sault in a year. The business started with nothing; we rented a little bachelor apartment across from the bus station and it served as an office and a crash space. Inside we had a phone, an answering machine, a desk, half a dozen chairs, an old chesterfield and a huge bed. The rudimentary kitchen included a working stove and fridge which was usually kept full of beer. One kitchen wall was covered with menus from the restaurants in town which delivered — no one cooked. We had three hookers on staff — Rita, an ex-stripper named Eve, and Terri, a woman who claimed to have been a madam in some other town. The stripper was the prettiest, Rita was willing to go anywhere and see anyone, the former madam promised to "throttle anyone who got out of hand." Alf ran errands for the service and drove the women to their dates. Before hiring me Alf spoke to the police about getting a licence for the service, but they said that wasn't necessary because escort services can't be licensed in the Sault. He then asked if he was breaking the law by starting his business and they told him they wouldn't bother him as long as no one complained. I couldn't believe his audacity.

The phone started ringing as soon as we placed our first ad. Callers asked for everything I would expect from Toronto callers. "No, we don't have a dungeon. No, we don't have any Asian women. No, we don't have any black women. Yes, she will do that, I'll send her right over." The stripper was turning two or three tricks a day at $150 a trick. Alf's girlfriend, Rita, was seeing five or six guys a day, sometimes more, but working her was a nightmare. She did anything with anybody for any amount of money. She'd show up at some guy's door, he'd tell her he only had fifty dollars (even though our standard rate was one-fifty and I always made that clear over the phone), she'd wave Alf off as if to say everything was cool, then turn the guy for fifty. Later Alf would tell me to let it go and not worry about the agency cut, which upset the other women.

A few customers complained about the former madam, Terri, saying she was either too rough or too uncooperative. "Yeah, I paid her, eh, but she wouldn't do anything for me. What kind of joint are you running anyway? I have a mind to call the cops. What you're doing is illegal you know." I turned these calls over to the boss. He told me to straighten things out with Terri. I confronted her after receiving my fifth or sixth complaint but she insisted all the complainers were liars and assholes. I reminded her that if she ever had a bad time with a customer she was to call me immediately and I'd send Alf over. Complaints dropped off after that.

We had a relaxed relationship with the Sault Ste. Marie police and not once during my time with Jean's did they bother us. I'm sure that every cop in town knew about our operation, just like everybody in Soo Michigan knew about Sneaky Pete's. The police could have made our lives very difficult, but we never gave them a reason to lean on us. The agency's women never made scenes regardless of where they went or who they saw (with the exception of Rita, but that problem was solved quietly and internally). No one from Jean's did anything out in the open that upset anyone's sense of propriety, so we were invisible. As long as we stayed invisible, the police were the least of our worries. This live-and-let-live attitude towards underground prostitution is pretty common in smaller cities.

Everything went well during the first couple of months. We were all making a few bucks and having a good time doing it. On quiet nights Alf would turn off the phone, order a couple of pizzas and we'd gorge ourselves on pepperoni and cheese while emptying the fridge of its beer. Rita warmed up to me even though I considered her the most unprofessional of the three pros, and an almost completely unreliable moneymaker. Whenever I sent her out on a date I could only guess at what she'd come back with. When I worked as a prostitute I hated surprises and I carried this prejudice with me when I began managing Alf's agency. It was one thing for me to worry about myself as I prepared for a client — I knew what I was and wasn't capable of — but worrying about three other women out on calls *I* had set up was far more stressful, and Rita proved adept at causing stress. Once she had money in her purse, she began drinking. If Rita wasn't on call, I didn't care how much she drank, but when she was working the drinking created a real problem.

I had a couple of long conversations with her and she eventually promised to settle down and work like a pro but I had my doubts. Not long afterwards I received a call from one of her regulars. In a voice filled with fear and spiced with anger he said she was lying on his bed "in a coma" and he didn't know what to do. I told him to do nothing but sit tight and someone would come over in a few minutes. I called Alf's pager and gave him the particulars. He went to the client's home and found Rita face down on the bed, out cold. She had passed out while working her way through a quart of Canadian Club given to her by the date. He explained to Alf the bottle of rye was cheaper than paying cash and that she had agreed to the deal. Alf loaded Rita into his van and drove her home. He also told her she was no longer employed.

Finding new women willing to work for the agency was easy; finding appropriate women was more difficult. One very attractive woman didn't realize she was applying for the job of prostitute. When I explained the nature of the work to her, she glared at me as if I were the resurrected mayor of Sodom and left. The No Drunks rule eliminated two more. Each interview was simple and took less than thirty minutes. If the woman knew what the job was about and looked and acted appropriately, all we had to discuss were the hours and days she was available. Any woman who could work from four in the afternoon until two in the morning was in. If during the interview I got the sense that I was talking to a drunk or a drug addict the woman was automatically rejected.

I hired two women to replace Rita, including the daughter of the former madam. The daughter said she was no stranger to the Business and claimed to have been turning tricks since she was sixteen. I had heard plenty of stories about mothers turning out their daughters but this was the first time I had ever met someone who said it had happened to her. She bore no ill feelings towards her mother and they always got along when they were in our small office. Terri denied she forced her child into prostitution but admitted her daughter had begun seeing men for money when she was eighteen, shortly after leaving high school. Both agreed the daughter never worked for the mother. I couldn't take the time to sort out the truth from the lies. The daughter was willing and able to work and she knew the score. I felt odd hiring her and even stranger sending her out on calls, knowing her mother knew what was going on, but the daughter proved to be competent and popular. She was comfortable with the work and only complained when our phone didn't ring.

I turned the occasional trick for Jean's myself. I took on the customers who were looking for something kinky because the other women were not interested in doing much more than straight sex. They all echoed Terri's opinion of activities like cross-dressing, bondage and domination when she announced, "That shit's too weird for me."

*   *   *

Not long after my meeting with Dorothy I met with my family doctor in the Sault, a woman I liked and trusted. I explained my feelings to her, feelings I had harboured for twenty years. I told her about my conversation with Dorothy and what I had learned from reading books on transsexualism. She was taken aback by what I told her and didn't know how to begin any sort of treatment or therapy, or even who to call for advice. I was prepared: I gave her photocopies of chapters from the books I'd read and articles dealing with treatment; names and phone numbers of gender identity clinics; a reading list — in short everything I had that I thought might be useful. I wanted to make it easy for her to help me. She promised to go through the material and get back to me as soon as she could. We met again a few days later and she asked me what I wanted her to do. I said I wanted her to prescribe estrogen, to develop female characteristics such as softer hair and skin as well as breasts. I knew that women in transition preparing for sex reassignment surgery (SRS) had to take estrogen for years and I thought, no time like the present to begin the process. Instead she gave me a prescription for Valium and referred me to a local psychiatrist.

The meeting with the shrink was no more fruitful. I gave him the identical package of material that I'd given my doctor and during our meeting I told him exactly the same things I told her. When he asked me what I expected of him, I talked about estrogen, quoting the articles which discussed the use of hormones in preparation for SRS. He approved of my Valium prescription and referred me to a psychologist for further counselling. I raised hell, arguing that I knew what was happening to me and that I didn't need counselling.

Nevertheless, once a week for a year I saw a counsellor, a young, studious-looking man who knew nothing about transition. Fifty-two conversations about life, family, sex, gender, prostitution — I tried to be honest and held nothing back. And week after week I would ask this man, "So what exactly are you going to do for me?"

"Help you reach a greater understanding about what you're going through and help you cope."

"I know what I'm going through and I am coping. All I need is a script for estrogen, let's say, two point five milligrams a day, and I'll be fine. I'll get out of your hair and you can spend your time talking to people who want to talk to you."

I didn't get a referral for hormone therapy. Instead he conducted question-and-answer sessions about my father. "I only see him two or three times a year. There's no problem." "Tell him about *this*? Are you kidding?"

I knew bugging my family doctor was unfair to her — transsexualism was out of her depth. The psychiatrist and the psychologist described me as an intelligent, highly informed patient, very knowledgeable about her "condition," but they didn't do a thing that I asked. Out of sheer frustration I began eating Valium like it was candy and that gave the psychologist something to grab onto; he had plenty of experience working with drug abusers. I took matters into my own hands and wrote to the gender-identity clinic at Toronto's Clarke Institute, explaining my situation. I also started buying birth-control pills which contained estrogen from my women friends in the Sault. This involved coming out to a small, select group of people, but I had spent so much time discussing transition with complete strangers in suits that I had grown numb to the idea of disclosure. The women were very supportive and before long I had plenty of estrogen, and none of my friends had to go without, thanks to a little double-doctoring. (Double-doctoring used to be easy: a patient would visit two different doctors and get the same prescription from each one. In recent years, computer networking and government crack-downs have made this practice more difficult.)

Estrogen didn't change my life. It didn't noticeably soften my skin, alter my voice, or give me hooters worthy of Hollywood. Taking estrogen did improve my mood and my self-esteem, however, and once I started popping birth-control pills I felt that I had taken my first real step on the journey of transition. I didn't care what the psychiatrist or psychologist thought; I had stepped out of their sphere of influence and I had found a reliable source for a drug which, at the time, was almost as vital to me as air and water.

The Clarke Institute's gender-identity clinic agreed to see me, provided I got a referral from a psychiatrist or a doctor. When I informed my shrink he phoned the Clarke immediately. He seemed relieved to be able to drop me from his case load, and I looked forward to dealing with people who knew something about what I was going through. I can't say that I saw light at the end of my tunnel but at least I felt my tunnel had an end. The need to get out of northern Ontario became a passion.

chapter 8

Soapboxes
On the Stroll

Once I realized there was absolutely no way I was going to resolve my gender dilemma in Sault Ste. Marie, I devoted all of my energies to returning to Toronto. I started keeping a journal and the more I wrote, the more I felt I had discovered what I really should be doing. But in the meantime, I needed to earn money in order to move south. I did a considerable amount of writing for a seedy collection of underground personal contact magazines published in Toronto by a young entrepeneur named Steve. I wrote tens of thousands of words of soft core pornography and was paid a bulk rate; thirty-five pages of "wall-to-wall" (simple stories that revolve solely around sex acts; no plot, plenty of description) earned me six hundred dollars. The subject matter was boring, the pay low, but I was getting paid to write and I was thrilled to see my name — even though it was a pseudonym — in a byline. I don't like pornography and I never wanted to write it, but every dollar I earned brought me one step closer to Toronto. By the spring of 1989 I had saved enough to leave the Sault.

Alf and the women of Jean's Escort Service were sorry to see me go, but no one was really surprised. They all thought I was leaving the Sault because of what happened in the Holiday Inn and I didn't feel like getting all heavy and telling them the truth. I never got too personal with Alf or any of the hookers, but they had all seen women in transition on American talk shows and I think everybody had put two and two together. They knew I was much more like one of the girls than one of the guys and that's how they always treated me. Even Alf, who was very much a regular guy, often referred to me as Mother. "Mother here looks after the girls and makes sure everybody stays out of trouble. I'm the boss but Mother runs the show." I liked that.

In July I moved in with my sister, but we both knew the arrangement was temporary. I needed to go back to hooking to support myself and working out of Tanya's home was impossible — she lived in a small apartment and there was no place for me to bring my dates. I told her about the prostitution and my transition. I had wanted to tell her about transition long before, but I didn't understand it well enough to explain it to someone else. Once I sorted everything out in my own mind, and worked up the nerve to come out, the telling was easy. Tanya took the news as well as I could have expected.

As we talked about prostitution, it became clear she was concerned for my safety, so we discussed AIDS, the cops and other dangers associated with the Biz. We didn't get into a heavy debate about the moral baggage connected with the sex trade. I don't know whether I convinced Tanya to look at prostitution as honest work, but I do think she started looking at the issue differently. For me the most important thing about the whole exchange was that Tanya's love for me didn't waiver. Explaining transition was more involved — Tanya wanted to understand and asked a lot of questions. She knew I would stop being a whore at some point in my life and even if she abhorred the idea all she had to do was tolerate it until I quit. Transition was a far weightier matter; I was redefining myself and the changes I talked about were permanent. Tanya did a marvellous job of grappling with it all, and I've never felt closer to her than I did once the telling was done.

Psychiatrists who work with women in transition would say this was when I truly began "living as a woman." But mistakes of perception happen all the time and still do. Depending upon how I dress or wear my hair I'll either get "sir-ed" or "ma'am-ed" from the strangers I deal with. If I think the interaction is important I'll correct any errors. If it's something inconsequential — "Excuse me sir, would you like fries or mashed…" — I don't bother. Women are expected to fit a stricter set of stereotypes than men and if some of us don't, we are assumed to be men, or at the very least lesbian. When I explain to someone whom I've just recently met that I am a woman, the new acquaintance is never surprised when he or she finds out I'm a lesbian. The message I get from them is that because I'm a woman who doesn't fit the mould I *must* be a dyke. When I confirm their suspicions, by doing something such as introduce Karen as my lover, they smile or nod knowingly

The following spring I found a suitable basement apartment on Arundel Street in Toronto's Greektown. The ads I placed in the weeklies attracted enough business for me to live on, but I didn't work the trade as hard as I did when I had started fifteen years previously. The attack I suffered in Sault Ste. Marie made me very cautious with new customers and I probably rejected many potential clients who might have been just fine. The Business had changed. In the seventies I expected my customers to treat me with some respect and I was seldom disappointed. Now, if a guy was kind or courteous he stood out like a rose in a parking lot. It's not that my customers were all mean and nasty, many were just cold and indifferent to what we were doing. I'm old-fashioned; I expect people to treat one another with courtesy and kindness regardless of what they're up to.

This change in the Biz is largely a result of the increased number of prostitutes. It's a buyer's market and a trick can be rude to a different woman every night for years. As women began undercutting each other, the prices for commercial sex began falling. One of the first rules I learned while working in retail sales was never to sell something too cheaply; if you do, your customers think your merchandise has little value. Customers, many of whom see hookers only as merchandise, began undervaluing the prostitutes and it became easier for them to treat their whores poorly. We've also become more tolerant of rudeness in our day-to-day lives. Sales clerks treat shoppers like nuisances. Good service in restaurants is becoming a rarity. Cabbies hardly ever offer to open doors or tote luggage. There's no service in the service industry and we've quietly accepted it.

Every stroll has at least one or two places where street prostitutes go to hang out while they're working. Women who work indoors can do a number of things to pass the time while they're waiting for their phones to ring. If nothing else, the TV is always there. The women who work the street don't have that option. Street work is hard and the hours can be long and boring. Bars and restaurants offer places where street prostitutes can take breaks and relax, get caught up on gossip and talk shop.

In Toronto, the best-known stroll is at Jarvis and Gerrard streets, just minutes away from Maple Leaf Gardens and the Eaton Centre. There are usually a dozen or so whores working this corner and on warm, busy summer nights I've seen over twenty women. The white women work the earlier shift, from eight to midnight, or up to bar closing. Later the black women predominate; they work from around eleven or midnight until four or five in the morning, depending on the flow of business and how well they break. At Church and Gerrard there is a licensed fast-food restaurant which stays open until the early hours of the morning. Attached to it is a small coffee shop which never closes. The people who run these businesses have a no-nonsense, neutral attitude to the trade which goes on around them, and to the women who work the corner. "You don't get in our face, we won't get in yours."

I started going to this coffee shop in the summer of 1989. I was working indoors at the time, both as an independent call-girl and for an escort service. Many escort-service managers frown on freelancers turning tricks on the side but Peter, the guy I worked for, had that old hippy, laid-back attitude that I associate with people who grew up in the 1960s. He just didn't care. On the days that I worked, I always stayed within earshot of my phone, but not every day was a working day. On good days, or nights, I'd make my money early and later in the evening I'd head downtown. More often than not around midnight or one in the morning I'd end up in the coffee shop or the restaurant at Church and Gerrard.

All sorts of people frequented the coffee shop or the restaurant late at night. Small-time drug dealers and their customers, many of them students from the nearby college residence, came and went. In the toilets hundreds of grams of cocaine were eagerly bought every week by our future corporate leaders. Every now and then a carload of drunken high-school kids from the suburbs would roll in, looking for coffee, food, or a little dope. The regular customers rarely paid any attention to these kids, whose desires usually exceeded their bankroll.

Next door to the restaurant was a well-known and popular gay bar jokingly referred to by many of its regulars as "the wrinkle room." The bar's clientele was older — not old by any means, but if a guy didn't look youthful enough to be somebody's younger brother he was old enough to be everybody's father. There was another bar located above the wrinkle room which catered to a younger crowd. The upper bar's dance floor was a little bigger, the lights were dimmer and the music was louder. Otherwise the two places were essentially the same. Young gay men didn't usually end up in the coffee shop, but wrinkle-room drinkers who couldn't find someone to go home with often came over for coffee. These older gay men were not as flamboyant as the younger guys and they didn't attract much attention from would-be gay bashers, many of whom, I suspect, stopped at the coffee shop to plan their attacks. The restaurant attracted the whole range of night people but the most intriguing to me were the downtown prostitutes.

I'd go to the coffee shop to write. I kept a journal in 1989 and found that I could spend long periods of time drinking coffee, smoking cigarettes and keeping up on my journal in the coffee shop. I talked with the other women about work, the weather, so-and-so's old man, whatever came to mind. A couple of years later I was still going into the same coffee shop but the talk had turned to prostitution politics, AIDS and safer sex. The most interesting nights I ever spent in the shop were during the summer of 1989.

Metro Toronto Police 52 Division patrolled the neighbourhood around the downtown stroll and it was not unusual to see a police cruiser pull up and park in front of the shop. One cop would saunter in to pick up coffee and doughnuts for himself and his partner while the other sat behind the wheel gazing around, looking kind of bored. The people who were known to the police — and wanted — would disappear into the washrooms. One or two conversations would stop, or the subjects would change in mid-sentence. Secretive phone calls would be cut short. The officer would nod and say hello to the whores he knew as he placed his order. The only people in the coffee shop who seemed genuinely pleased to see the police were the employees working the counter. The waitress would always give the cop the best doughnuts and the freshest coffee and contrary to popular belief, the cops always paid, at least when I was watching. As the police car pulled away life would quickly return to normal. The same routine would be followed if an undercover officer walked into the place. Narcs and plainclothed cops may look a little different but more often than not they were just as obvious as the harness bulls.

I rarely saw a prostitute get arrested right on the stroll; that's not how the police work. Undercover cops would usually entice the women to get into their cars and then arrest them a few minutes later, once they had driven away from the area. But one night it was different. I was sitting near the front window watching the street; a couple of women were at a nearby table, smoking, drinking, and complaining about how quiet the night was. Across the street a young, thin black woman was working hard trying to pull a date. The couple of white girls she shared the sidewalk with watched her with disinterested eyes — it's tough getting enthusiastic about the work on a slow night.

A white, 52 Division cruiser pulled up and stopped in front of the black woman. No one in the coffee shop paid much attention to this. We all expected to see the woman lean into the passenger window as the cops inside questioned her. The cop on the passenger side of the car got out and started to talk to her. She suddenly tried to get away from him, but he was too fast. The cop, who was much bigger than the prostitute, snatched her by the arm and pulled her into him. She struggled for a second or two, then gave up. By this time we were all watching. The cop took the woman around the back of the car, as if he planned to slide her in through the rear door on the driver's side. We could see his mouth moving the whole time, but we had no idea what he was saying to her. Then she said something to him and it must've really pissed him off. Without warning he slammed her head against the solid part of the car frame which supports the roof. He smashed her head against it, over and over, until she went limp. He then opened the rear door and carelessly laid her onto the seat. He rejoined his partner in the front and the car pulled away. The whole incident took less than a minute.

As the cruiser drove out of sight, I wondered if the young woman had a child at home. Pamela George had two. Recently (January 1997), we watched on the news as two middle-class white men — one a university basketball star — were convicted of manslaughter and sentenced to 6 ½ years each for the beating death of Ms. George, a Native woman who was working as a prostitute. The judge in the case told the jury that a first degree murder conviction, which would have carried much stiffer penalties, would be "dangerous" because Ms. George "was indeed a prostitute." She had performed oral sex on the two men before they beat her and there was some debate about whether or not she had consented to the sex. The judge seemed to think this was relevant. Pamela George was victimized many times over — by the society in which she lived that denies so much to its Native population, by the men who killed her, by a judicial system that thought their crime was mitigated by the fact of her profession, and by rampant sexism. As Chief Lindsay Kaye remarked upon hearing the verdict, "It gives the right to anybody to go give a woman a beating."

Those of us in the coffee shop who had watched the police assault were speechless. The white women who had been working alongside the black pro were gone. The cops were gone. Moments after the attack the street was quiet and relatively peaceful, as if nothing unusual or violent had happened. The flow of traffic moved by smoothly but no one was slowing down — there was no reason to shop, there was nothing to see. The women at the nearby table finally began talking and speculating about who the woman was. Why was she grabbed off the street? What would happen to her now? Will she be all right? I couldn't overhear everything they were saying but I thought they might have known what was going on. I asked them why a cop would beat up a woman like that.

"Because she's just a 'ho.'" The expression on the woman's face and the tone of her voice said it all.

I was never able to discover what happened to the arrested woman, but it was clear that the two cops knew they could get away with their actions. No one would do anything, no one would remember anything. I had never witnessed such a scene before. Working inside isolated me from much of the dangers of prostitution. I had heard plenty of stories, I had seen the black eyes and the broken teeth, but this was different. It had happened right in front of me and the attacker wasn't some drunk trick or pissed-off boyfriend — those somehow would've been a little easier to handle. The attacker was a cop and that made me feel just that much more vulnerable and helpless.

I left the shop but I couldn't stop thinking about what I had seen. I couldn't shake the sick feeling I had in my stomach. It took me a few days to get the images of the attack out of my mind and it was some time before I turned another trick.

I had heard stories about police abusing prostitutes. I had been ignored by the police myself when I tried to lay charges against the trick who beat me up in Sault Ste. Marie. But I had always thought these were isolated incidents. Now I knew better. I decided that it was time for me to get political about the work.

The debate over prostitutes' rights exploded in the 1970s as whores started to organize themselves. In 1973 a rights group called COYOTE (Call Off Your Old Tired Ethics) was formed in San Francisco and within months similar organizations sprang up all over the United States. Many of these groups did not last long, but COYOTE stayed. A year later in Lyons, France, a group of fifty prostitutes, community activists, lawyers and journalists staged a protest during which they demanded an end to police repression, harassment and brutalization of whores. The police in Lyons responded by cracking down on prostitution. The pros staged more protests and the police toughened their crackdown. The battle between the cops and the pros reached a turning point on June 3, 1975, when somewhere between 100 to 150 prostitutes occupied the church of St. Nizier, in the centre of Lyons. The women hung a banner over the façade of the church: *Nos enfants ne veulent pas leurs mères en prison* (Our children don't want their mothers in prison) and appealed to the public for support. The public did come out in support of the women and the French media broadcast the event all over France. In a show of solidarity, prostitutes occupied churches in three other French cities and staged strikes in three more. Parisienne hookers occupied the St. Bernard Chapel in Montparnasse and by this time the prostitute activists had caught the attention of the world's press. On June 11 the cops moved in and cleared the hookers out of all the occupied churches but the ideas that inspired the activism had solidified and later that year the French Collective of Prostitutes was formed. The English Collective of Prostitutes (modelled after the French collective) was formed shortly after as an independent organization within the International Wages for Housework Campaign. The prostitutes' rights movement was in full swing.

Feminists have not decided how to respond to prostitution. In the 1960s it was fashionable to condemn the sex trade and pity the women working in it. Prostitution was cited as an example of the male oppression of women and the call went out for its abolition. As feminists grappled with the issue of prostitution, other questions surfaced. Is prostitution a form of sexual expression and, if so, are women limiting their forms of expression by condemning the Business? Are prostitutes more sexually liberated because they are willing to profit by exploiting their own sex and sexuality? Prostitution is a way for women to earn money so should prostitution issues be considered labour issues? Should prostitution be considered a freedom of choice issue, as is abortion?

By the 1980s, two separate camps had formed. Many traditional feminists wanted prostitution abolished. In the other camp women argued that prostitution was honest work and should be treated as such. Others felt whores were sexually liberated women. Advocates of freedom of choice stated that women should be able to do what they wanted with their bodies. None of this made much of a difference to most of the prostitutes I've met.

In Canada there is no on-going relationship between prostitutes and the women's movement, and the two feminist camps have stayed apart. In 1986 the Canadian Organization for the Rights of Prostitutes (CORP) tabled an emergency resolution at the National Action Committee (NAC) on the Status of Women's annual meeting, asking the organization to oppose "any and all legislation which seeks to limit the personal and business lives of adult prostitutes." The resolution was passed, but with great difficulty. Since the late eighties NAC has advised women to look favourably on politicians who support the decriminalization of voluntary, adult prostitution, but NAC is not in the trenches fighting for decriminalization — no mainstream feminist organization is.

In 1987 CORP formed the Citizens' Organization to Repeal Prostitution-Related Laws (the name was later changed to the Campaign to Decriminalize Prostitution or CDP), an organization where pros and non-prostitutes could work together to change our prostitution laws. The CDP was a terrific idea, but it fell apart in less than two years. Prostitutes alone don't have enough influence; they have to involve other citizens in the movement to prove to our lawmakers that their goals have widespread support. CDP collapsed because the initial organizers refused to allow full participation to non-prostitute members. The irony is that political prostitutes complain when mainstream organizations discuss prostitution without inviting pros to take part. The whores who organized CDP, a citizens' organization, barred ordinary people from their place at the table.

The Elizabeth Fry Society, a social service agency which works with women in trouble with the law, called for decriminalization in the mid-1970s but Canadian whores didn't start organizing until the 1980s. The Association for the Safety of Prostitutes (ASP) was founded by Marie Arrington and Sally de Quadros in 1982 and ASP was active in Vancouver, where it held its first Hooker Pride march in 1982. In 1984 it occupied a church to protest an injunction which banned prostitutes from Vancouver's west end. In Toronto and Montreal we've seen the level of violence inflicted on prostitutes go up when they were singled out as targets by residents groups. According to Marie Arrington of ASP, following the passing of the injunction in Vancouver there was a dramatic increase in the level of violence directed against that city's hookers. CORP, like so many grass-roots political organizations, was formed out of anger — founder Peggy Miller was sick and tired of getting busted. I only met Peggy once, briefly, during my career but she was a legend. She had done it all — walked the streets and gotten busted, worked as a call-girl and gotten busted, ran a brothel and gotten busted. By 1983 she was fed up and began campaigning on her own to have Canada's prostitution laws wiped out. Miller's friends advised her she would have a better chance of being heard and achieving her goal if she created an organization and surrounded herself with like-minded people. She would have more credibility and a larger presence in the eyes of the public, the media, and ultimately the federal government. Miller took this advice and CORP was born that same year.

CORP consistently dismissed the efforts of ASP and the group which grew out of ASP, POWER (Prostitutes and Other Women for Equal Rights), saying these groups portrayed prostitutes as victims and wanted to see prostitution elimi-nated. ASP and POWER spokespeople have said if women had the same economic choices as men, fewer women would turn to prostitution out of economic necessity — which is true. ASP, POWER, CORP and later Maggie's did all have one major thing in common — they all wanted prostitution decriminalized. Decriminalization should not be confused with legalization. If prostitution were legalized, our existing set of laws would be replaced by a new set. Decriminaliza-tion would result in the removal of existing laws from the Criminal Code; no new prostitution laws would replace them. ASP and POWER argued that this change would give women more control over their bodies while other solutions, leading to the eventual elimination of prostitution, were worked out. Decriminalization would remove one level of the victimization of prostitutes — the victimization they suffer at the hands of the criminal justice system. An ASP booklet states, "We will not eliminate prostitution until all members of our society have a way to support themselves, and all have control over their lives and bodies." If prostitution were decriminalized in Canada it would be easier for women to leave the Business. Until it becomes as easy for women to leave the trade as it is for them to get into it, prostitution will always be with us.

CORP, on the other hand, is not interested in seeing prostitution eliminated. CORP supports decriminalization, which will allow prostitutes to work how and where they like, providing they abide by municipal zoning bylaws regulating commercial activity. According to CORP, it is not the business of prostitution which victimizes whores, but the criminal justice system. CORP believes this change in the laws would go a long way towards destigmatizing prostitutes, since they would no longer be seen as criminals.

Unlike ASP and later POWER, CORP was not formed to provide any kind of service. CORP is a lobby group and its sole reason for existence is to campaign for a change in our laws. Membership in CORP was and is supposed to be restricted to working prostitutes, but exceptions have always been made. If someone wanted to get involved, she had to meet with the other members and be approved. It was all reminiscent of the new kid on the block trying to join a club or gang. If everyone liked you, you were in; if not, you were out. When CORP was trying to fatten up its membership list, Peggy Miller's friend Chris Bearchell was made an honorary member, even though she had never worked as a whore. It was questionable whether Gwendolyn, a Toronto stripper who later became a performance artist, had ever turned a trick, but she too was allowed to join.

Another champion of decriminalization was the Toronto Prostitutes' Community Service Project, better known as Maggie's. Maggie's was conceived sometime in the mid-1980s. Some say it was gay-activist-turned-prostitute Danny Cockerline who first came up with the idea to pay prostitutes to teach other prostitutes about AIDS and safer sex, and to teach the public about the realities of prostitution. Others say Maggie's was Valerie Scott's idea; she often told me how, in the early eighties, she handed out business cards with safe-sex information printed on them to women working the streets of Toronto. Regardless of whose brainchild Maggie's was, money was a key aspect of the idea. Valerie Scott, Danny Cockerline, Gwendolyn and Chris Bearchell, all involved at the beginning, wanted to get paid for doing what a few had already been doing for free, and the three levels of government were all seen as possible funding sources. CORP's founder, Peggy Miller, predicted that an influx of money would cause no end of trouble and cautioned her activist friends to that effect, but her warnings were ignored.

I found CORP's phone number in one of those left-wing, tabloid-sized newspapers that you can find in community centre lobbies or trendy book stores and was invited to meet the inner circle at an Indian restaurant a week or so later. I arrived at the small west-end Toronto restaurant early and passed the time nursing a drink while the staff rearranged the tables to accommodate our group. As the late afternoon melded into early evening the others slowly trickled in. The first to arrive were Valerie Scott and Ryan Hotchkiss of CORP. Valerie was a scrawny, pale-skinned woman in her mid-thirties, her juvenile-looking body topped with a mane of curly brown hair. She was a freelance call-girl but no one would have guessed her profession merely by looking at her. She wore an over-sized workshirt stuffed into a pair of tight-fitting, tattered blue jeans; her make-up was minimal. Black cowboy boots worn over her pant legs completed the sort of sixties look. Ryan, Valerie's lover, was also a thin, pale thirty-something-year-old woman dressed as casually as CORP's frontperson, and she looked surprisingly boyish. Even her straight blonde hair was cut short and worn in a more masculine than feminine style. We exchanged hellos and intros, then chatted about what brought me there while we waited for the rest of the party to show up.

I explained how I had read about the existence of a number of prostitutes' right groups while living in northern Ontario. We discussed my past experiences in prostitution while Valerie sussed out my knowledge, opinions and beliefs about the work — Ryan remained quiet for the most part. Valerie had the pros' rights mantra down cold, but when Ryan jumped into the conversation her comments were better thought out and her questions were more penetrating. Valerie may have been CORP's public persona, but I felt Ryan had a better understanding of the ins and outs of prostitution.

Before long we were joined by four women, all of them involved in some way with Maggie's and CORP. The unofficial leader of the foursome was Christine Bearchell, a self-described "gay woman" who insisted she be referred to as Chris. Chris — who dressed in the shabbiest of clothes, weighed in at well over 250 pounds and stood not much more than five feet tall — was no prostitute but that didn't stop her from playing a key role in Maggie's. She was the group's administrator. Bearchell's claim to fame was as a gay activist and journalist, having worked for *The Body Politic* before a long, involved court battle bankrupted the magazine and knocked her out of a job. Chris was an advocate of prostitutes' rights and sexual freedom and I got the impression that as far as sex between two consenting adults went, she harboured no taboos.

Gwendolyn, performance artist and part-time stripper, was Maggie's best-known street outreach worker. Three or four nights a week she rode a ramshackle old bike around Toronto's downtown strolls, handing out condoms to anyone who would take them and delivering a rudimentary safe-sex message to anyone who would listen. Gwendolyn prided herself on knowing every girl on the street as well as most of the guys, but I later learned that very few people, except perhaps Chris Bearchell, really knew Gwendolyn. She was thin, small and odd. Her size and shape reminded me of an Olympic gymnast but her short, mousy brown hair gave away her age; she was in her late thirties. She and I were probably the oldest people at the table.

Two other women accompanied Bearchell — her lover, Irit, and one member of Maggie's Board of Directors; neither were prostitutes. I was surprised that of the four Maggie's people I met that night, only one might have worked as a prostitute, and that was more than ten years ago. Maggie's always claimed to be an organization controlled and run by prostitutes, so where were the whores?

The evening flowed smoothly once the formalities were taken care of. The atmosphere was casual and pleasant. I knew I was being checked out, but everyone seemed comfortable with my views on prostitution and AIDS. I felt I could work with these people if given the chance and everyone at the table made it clear that the chance would come. I was excited when I finally left the restaurant hours later, confident that I would have the opportunity to get directly involved in something I felt strongly about. What I did not pick up on were the undercurrents of mistrust, animosity and jealousy that flowed under the table, undercurrents that would eventually rip apart both groups and destroy friendships.

Once I became a CORP member it wasn't long before I became a player in the group. I would have been satisfied answering phones or writing letters, but Valerie thought I could prove more useful as a spokesperson. I had never done this sort of thing but 1989 seemed to be my year for doing things I had never done before so I accepted the position. I wondered what would I do: Talk with college students writing papers on prostitution? Speak at the occasional community meeting? I wish! I was astonished to learn that my first gig was to appear before the federal government's Justice Committee to argue against the communicating law. When Bill C-49, which led to the creation of the communicating law, was passed in 1984 the House added the stipulation that the law would be reviewed in five years' time to determine its impact on street prostitution. The committee had summoned the usual suspects to talk about the law and street prostitution and whores were being represented by POWER and CORP. Valerie, Ryan and I made up the CORP contingent and we received our invitation less than twenty-four hours before we were scheduled to appear. We madly dashed around trying to get ready and flew into Ottawa late that night. To make matters worse we were slated to speak early the following morning.

Valerie had no use for anyone involved with POWER and I thought it was ironic that on our way to the committee meetings we had to take the same elevator as the POWER delegates. We weren't in that creaky old box for more than a minute or two when Valerie got into verbal fisticuffs. However, always mindful of the presence of the media, when the elevator doors opened, she calmly stepped out as though nothing was wrong. We spent an hour waiting for our turn to speak. I didn't know what to expect. I believed that the communicating law was wrong, but I wasn't a street prostitute and I hadn't had time to work out my arguments. Valerie had lectured me on the evils of the prostitution laws, but her points were superficial and seemed to be geared towards two-minute television interviews. I agreed with everything she said, but I wanted something with a little more depth. When a parliamentary official invited us into the committee room, I went in cold, and scared to death.

Valerie was the lead singer in our little band and Ryan and I filled in the gaps. Our presentation, which took about half an hour, was followed by a question-and-answer session and here we all did well. The Justice Committee was made up of members from all three political parties, and, although we expected to gather most of our support from the Liberal and NDP members, the Tories asked the most intelligent questions. (The award for the dumbest question asked went to former Liberal MP John Nunziata, who, thinking I was a man, asked me if I had many female customers.)

The Conservatives could see prostitution as a business and they questioned us accordingly, asking about things like

income, expenses and taxes. (The two most common questions asked pros are, "Do you enjoy it?" and "Do you pay
taxes?") The committee members were surprised to learn
that we did indeed pay income taxes. I filed as a prostitute
for years. I usually listed my occupation as "escort" but
during those years when I was particularly upset with our
government I filed as "WHORE!" Revenue Canada took my
money either way. I won't guess the percentage of pros who
pay their taxes faithfully; I suspect many do not. I have
known many prostitutes who paid taxes yearly because they
owned property or had built up extensive financial paper
trails through investments and the use of credit. These
women, like so many other Canadians, feared being audited
by Revenue Canada, so they always paid up come April.

We left the meeting feeling cautiously optimistic and for
a few days we thought the communicating law might be
struck down, something we would have considered a major
victory, but while we spoke against the law, arguing it was
ineffective and unconstitutional, others such as Art Eggleton
(Toronto's mayor at the time) and June Rowlands (chair of
the Metro Toronto Police Commission) argued that the law
was too lenient. In June 1990, the Supreme Court of Canada
upheld the law by a vote of four to two. The four judges
who approved of the law agreed that it limited the right to
freedom of expression guaranteed by the Charter of Rights
but said the limit was reasonable and justified in a free and
democratic society.

Valerie took the Supreme Court decision very hard, but
all it told me was that CORP's fight had just begun. In time I
became CORP's primary spokesperson and the most publicly
vocal prostitute in Canada. My work as a pro turned into a

sideline as I became more involved as an activist and began writing seriously about prostitution issues. As I gained more and more personal satisfaction from writing, and less and less from whoring, it became inevitable that I would soon leave the Business for good.

chapter 9

And the Band
Plays On
and On ...

Prostitutes had been insisting on protected sex with customers long before the emergence of AIDS; no pro looked forward to an unplanned pregnancy and there were plenty of other sexually transmitted diseases she had to protect herself from. If you caught something you went to a doctor, got a shot or a prescription, and that was that. Regulars were often allowed to "ride bareback" because after turning a guy a few times you thought you could size him up pretty well. "Yes, he's nice enough, and he seems clean." Certain sexually transmitted diseases (STDs) reveal themselves on close examination: if you didn't see anything dripping, weeping or flaring up, odds were the guy wasn't carrying anything. Not so with someone who is HIV positive. AIDS changed everything. It changed the relationships between prostitutes and their clients, between prostitutes and the community and among prostitutes themselves. Everyone involved in the Business was affected.

AIDS delivered a weapon into the hands of everyone involved in prostitution and that weapon was fear. When I began working there were prostitutes who didn't care whether or not their customers used protection, but these risk takers were in the minority. AIDS made safer sex a matter of life and death and condom use, especially with new customers, was standard in the industry. Rubbers do more than protect prostitutes from reckless, disease-carrying customers, they act as intimacy barriers. When you earn a living by having meaningless sex with strangers, it's nice to have something physical that differentiates the commercial sex from the recreational, and from private, intimate lovemaking. The latex prevents that most precious part of the client from coming into contact with that most private part of the prostitute. There's sex, then there's *sex*, then there's making love. Customers get sex.

According to the Museum of Contraception (run by the Ortho-McNeil company in Ontario), men have been sheathing their penises in an effort to avoid STDs at least since the days of the pharoahs. In the mid-1500s Gabriel Fallopius designed a sheath that went over the tip of a penis and under the foreskin. It was held in place by a pink ribbon in the hope that it would appear more attractive to women. In the 1600s England's King Charles II asked his physician, the Earl of Condom, to come up with something to protect him from syphillis. The earl devised an oiled sheath made from sheep intestine and soon all the noblemen were wearing them, but they reused their sheaths without washing them. Syphillis took its toll. A condom made of vulcanized rubber appeared in the 1870s but it wasn't thin or disposable. Men were instructed to wash their rubbers before and after intercourse and use the same ones until they cracked or tore. These early condoms were effective but unpopular. Thinner, latex condoms weren't introduced until the 1930s.

Ever since condoms were invented, there have been men who didn't want to use them. These days you can often find these guys in singles bars; they're the customers with handfuls of money trying to buy their way out of wearing the loathed latex. They offer their whores an extra twenty dollars or so in the hope that they'll be allowed to dispense with the rubber and they often accompany their pitches with lines like, "You don't have to worry about me, I'm clean. I'm a married man." Marriage has never made anyone immune to sexually transmitted diseases and if I had a buck for every hooker who caught something from a "clean," married man I could retire tomorrow — comfortably. In recent years many prostitutes have begun to use condoms consistently with both their customers and their personal partners. When they explain to their customers why condom use is necessary, most get the message, but the young ones, the indestructable ones, continue as if nothing has changed. It's a gay disease or a junkie's disease, so they think. But prostitutes *are* concerned — they don't want to be infected by their dates.

If an AIDS 101 lecture doesn't convince a customer to wear a condom, a pro can use another tactic. "Look honey, I understand I don't have to worry about you, you being a clean, married man and all, but you don't know anything about me or the other guys I've slept with. You're not the only one who doesn't like using latex; who knows, maybe I caught something from somebody else." A woman is approximately three times more likely to be infected by having sex with an HIV positive man than a man is by having straight sex with an HIV positive woman. This is crucial to all women, but it won't deter a stubborn customer — he doesn't care about the whore.

Oral sex has become immensely popular since the onset of AIDS. For years the general public was unsure whether unprotected oral sex was as risky as unprotected vaginal or anal sex, but the medical profession and the gay community now both seem to think it is less risky. Hard-pressed hookers who don't want to engage in unprotected vaginal sex can offer the oral alternative and feel less threatened. Stubborn whores like me who insist the guys wear condoms all the time can still give satisfaction. Sex with a condom may not be the same as sex without, but a lot can be done with hands, lips and tongue — all it takes is willingness and a little imagination.

As I worked through the eighties and early nineties I assumed all of my customers were veritable hot zones of infectious disease and my caution paid off — I never caught an STD. Once I began working in the AIDS business, I learned that there were still prostitutes willing to take chances if the money was right. A few of these pros didn't seem to care what happened to them, but the majority were afraid of the possible consequences of engaging in risky behaviour. Frightened or not, everyone knew how the AIDS virus was transmitted and they knew what would happen if they got infected. Low self-esteem wasn't the main reason why some pros took risk money, economic pressure was. As the Business changed from the 1970s to the 1990s, it became more difficult to make a living selling sex. For the destitute pro working North Regent Park or Parkdale the opportunity to earn an extra twenty dollars was, and is, a powerful incentive. However, the prostitute population in Canada has not been decimated by AIDS — stark proof that whores working in the eighties were doing something right.

The effect AIDS had on how prostitutes relate to each other was subtle, but real. Street prostitutes traditionally worked in small groups of two or more, so that the women could watch out for each other. After the federal government toughened up the laws against street prostitution in 1984 the women spread out over existing strolls, or moved around and created new ones, in order to appear less visible to the police. But this made them more vulnerable to all forms of harassment. Anti-prostitute campaigns directed at customers were being launched. Health departments told men that hiring prostitutes was dangerous. Residents groups told customers to stay out of their neighbourhoods. Police departments continued sweeping prostitutes but they turned their attentions to customers as well. Demand always exceeds supply in this Business, but some strolls grew quiet while others stayed busy.

AIDS did not reduce the number of street prostitutes and at times the competition among them got fierce as they tried to cope with the pressure. Women fought over choice corners and other spots on busy streets, or put the word out that so-and-so was HIV positive. The rumours were often ignored, but other times supposedly infected women were ostracized by their peers or even attacked — having HIV positive women on the street was bad for business. If regular customers picked up on the rumours, they ignored the pros in question and moved on to others. Some abandoned the street altogether and turned to escort services and call-girls. Street rumours are virtually impossible to effectively quash, so the only thing the accused whores could do was take their business to another stroll, or to another town. When I did AIDS outreach, nobody discussed their HIV status unless it was to tell me they weren't positive. People were reluctant to visit clinics known for doing AIDS testing for fear of picking up the stigma of being HIV positive. Those who *were* HIV positive were reluctant to seek treatment for the same reason, but without information, medication and support an HIV positive person could get sick sooner, and if she or he stayed on the street the word got out anyway. The stigma of being HIV positive ruined the lives of many people living in mainstream society — the stigma was just as damaging to those living close to the fringe.

Prostitutes' rights activists knew they had to do something to counter the lies and hysteria being generated around AIDS and prostitution. They knew pros had to shake the Typhoid Mary stigma and they also wanted to ensure that new people coming into the Business learned how to protect themselves from STDs. In the past, inexperienced pros learned the tricks of the trade from those with experience, but the networks were breaking down and HIV/AIDS was an evolving illness. Prostitutes needed a steady flow of accurate, up-to-date information in order to protect themselves.

Maggie's is often described as Canada's first peer education project set up by and for prostitutes, though, technically speaking, prostitutes have never formed the majority of its board. The first time I attended a Maggie's board meeting I sat in as an observer from CORP. Valerie Scott and Ryan Hotchkiss invited me, board president June Callwood welcomed me — I was impressed. A month later Valerie Scott recommended the board take me on and June Callwood made the formal motion. I was elected! I knew nothing about being a board member but I felt I could learn the ropes as I went along. At times I was disappointed with myself because I wanted to do more than just get together with a dozen people once a month and yak about prostitution. Everyone knew I wanted to get more involved and as luck would have it a staff position opened up in the spring of 1990, and I was hired.

Maggie's paid its staff well, particularly when our salaries were compared to those paid by other community-based agencies. A full-time employee earned $36,000 a year — good money for a job that often entailed working less than thirty hours a week. There were two job classifications at Maggie's: project administrator (Chris Bearchell) and outreach workers (everyone else). We were supposed to contact other pros, either by talking with them on the street or calling the numbers they published in their ads, and encourage them to practice safe sex at work and at home. We were also supposed to act as walking repositories of information on all sexually transmitted diseases and we always had condoms and clean needles to give to those who wanted them. I did plenty of street outreach while I was with Maggie's but I considered telephone outreach to be a waste of time. It smacked of AIDS telemarketing and having worked for so long as an escort I knew how annoying these kind of calls could be.

On the surface, doing street outreach for Maggie's was easy. I'd fill up a big purse or bag with condoms and needles then go out onto the street and give them away to hookers, customers and anyone else who wanted them. I had to have a working knowledge of AIDS and other STDs just in case someone asked me a question like, "I heard douching with Coca-Cola kills the AIDS virus. Is that true?"

"No."

"Uh-oh!"

I was supposed to work the same strolls night after night so the pros got to know me and would talk to me about AIDS, their boyfriends, the cops, bad dates — anything. I was also supposed to talk prostitution politics and encourage the women to organize and stand up for their rights, or at least get involved with Maggie's.

I would go out around ten or eleven, not too early but not so late as to be bothering the women while they worked through the bar rush. Moving the condoms was a snap; everybody took handfuls provided they liked the brands I was carrying. Experienced prostitutes always have their personal preferences and they weren't interested in unknown or unreliable rubber. Maggie's usually got its condoms from Toronto's Department of Health and every once in a while they'd toss us a few cases of garbage condoms, ones that had reputations for leaking or not staying on, and these I literally could not give away. The offer of needles ("fits") made some women uncomfortable, but before long I knew who the junkies were and I offered fits only to them.

Getting to know the women was easy because they were usually friendly and chatty and very familiar with outreach workers prowling downtown. On any given night the downtown hookers could be showered with condoms, needles, bleach kits, coffee, sandwiches, pamphlets, advice, counselling, referrals, offers of places to stay and the Word of God from the likes of Maggie's, The Works, The Street Patrol, Street Outreach Services, Youthlink Innercity, Covenant

House and The Salvation Army. The agencies rarely stag-
gered their times on the stroll; at ten in the evening
(Monday to Friday; they didn't work weekends) pros could
easily get all kinds of free goodies. At two in the morning a
prostitute couldn't score a condom from a social worker to
save her life.

As I watched the parade of agency vans, motor homes,
and sidewalk-bound outreach workers pass by on the street I
often felt redundant. All I offered were condoms, fits and
conversation, with no strings attached, but the women
always seemed glad to see me and they always cleaned me
out. I never insisted that any woman come by the drop-in or
take a pamphlet. Here are your condoms, want to talk about
anything ... no ... okay, see you later. Most women did want
to talk and whenever I went out I made sure I took plenty of
coffee money. This was essential because we gabbed over java
in late-closing fast-food restaurants, away from the noise and
the often bitter cold of the street. I listened to hundreds of
stories, the majority of them sad or mundane.

I give a half-deck of smokes to the woman with the black
eye trying to decide if she wants to turn the guy in or live
with the battering because she loves him. I couldn't tell her
what to do but I remind her of her options. I share a coffee
with a young prostitute who is up on her third communicating bust and is looking at doing time.

Then there's the single mother, hooking to supplement
her welfare cheque, who is terrified of being arrested for
soliciting because she thinks the Children's Aid will snatch
away her kid if they find out.

"And they always find out," offers another pro who is
able to see the darkest side of anything.

A third woman throws her opinion in. "We're out here trying to put food on the table and if Children's Aid gets wind they say we're unfit mothers and take away our babies. What do they think, that we're out here partying?" It's unanimous, all the women hate Children's Aid.

I hated running into women with problems because often there was little, if anything, I could do. Outreach workers quickly have to develop thick skins and learn how to cope with feelings of helplessness. There were nights when I wondered why I bothered going out at all.

The street outreach was valuable but not just because we were able to pass on information and AIDS prevention paraphernalia; the street repaid our charity by providing us with a wealth of information we couldn't have gotten anywhere else, about prostitutes and drugs, for example. Very few pros took the needles I offered and this contradicted everything I had heard about street prostitutes and drug addiction. If most pros were junkies, hooking to feed drug habits, why did I have such a hard time getting rid of clean, brand new fits? Even the women who came to know me on a first-name basis weren't interested in scoring needles from me. I looked around for answers. One theory was that women didn't want to get busted while carrying drug paraphernalia, the possession of which is a criminal offence. (Outreach workers who walked or drove around with bags of fits to give away were technically breaking the law but the narcs never bothered us; who says the cops can't practice selective enforcement?) But this theory didn't make sense. Cocaine injectors hit up often and go through plenty of needles while on a run. An addicted coke banger can go through a handful of needles in no time, so carrying fits around for a few hours isn't an issue for them. A heroin addict doesn't use as many needles in a day as a coke injector, but in 1990 needles were hard to come by unless you had a prescription for an injectable medication such as insulin. Heroin addicts greedily accepted free needles handed out with no questions asked. There was also an economic incentive to take the needles — they were worth money on the street. A clean syringe could fetch two bucks from someone wired to an injectable drug. Still, I could go out night after night and hand out hundreds of condoms but not give away a single needle.

The whole idea of giving needles to people on the street was a contentious one for Maggie's. The reason for doing so was straightforward enough: giving drug users clean fits is a way to reduce the spread of AIDS. Sharing a contaminated needle is a very effective way to transmit the HI-virus; if drug injectors use clean needles every time they hit up, the chances of spreading the virus around are greatly reduced. So where do drug users get clean fits on the street when they have no money? — from someone like a Maggie's outreach worker. However, half the staff didn't want to give out needles because they feared we would be upholding the stereotype that all whores are junkies. Oddly enough no one thought that by giving hookers condoms we were implying that they didn't practice safe sex.

Needle distribution and needle exchange were hot political potatoes in 1990 and Toronto's Board of Health wanted the agencies involved to keep accurate records on how many fits they gave out and took in. The board felt it could use this information to more accurately estimate the number of people injecting drugs. Many people at Maggie's just didn't want to bother with the paperwork, but others wanted nothing to do with junkies. It made no difference what kind of drug you injected or how often; if you put a needle in your arm without a doctor's permission you were a junkie. Junkies were trouble, loose cannons, wild cards.

Another bone of contention was whether we should have been distributing needles or exchanging clean ones for dirty ones. Projects like Toronto's The Works ran a needle exchange — a user gave The Works ten dirty needles and got ten clean ones in return. Many people feared that the free distribution of needles, rather than an exchange, would mean more needles on the street and more people shooting drugs. Maggie's never resolved this question while I was there. It was left up to each staff member as to whether they carried, distributed or exchanged needles. I thought this was a cop-out, but others were happy — they no longer had to deal with needles, or the people who used them.

Maggie's outreach workers were often asked for things such as a quiet place where someone could unwind after a rough date, a place where people could meet and talk without entertaining curious onlookers, or somewhere to hide from a drunken boyfriend. Maggie's had long wanted a drop-in and resource centre and in the summer of 1990 we opened one in the heart of Cabbagetown. Similar organizations had already established prostitute drop-in centres in at least two Canadian cities. Winnipeg's centre had a washer and dryer available for its clients, as well as the usual collection of STD information. Stepping Stone, a Halifax-based project run by a group of former and currently working prostitutes and social workers, opened a similar drop-in and, according to the staff people I've met, it's popular among Halifax's hookers. Maggie's original goal was to emulate these drop-ins, then go a little further. Chris and Gwendolyn wanted the space to feel like a clubhouse. We all liked the idea of having a washer and dryer available for our visitors, many of whom were homeless. Board president June Callwood often talked about setting up some form of child care for pros, sort of a night-care centre, but her idea never got off the ground.

We set up in a second storey walk-up over a convenience store, located on what is part of the North Regent Park stroll. The space wasn't chosen because of the suitability of the location, which was far from ideal, but because of the low rent. Wages sucked up most of Maggie's funding, so everything else was done on the cheap. Chris put together a small office where she stored our computer and the reams and reams of paper required to support the project. The rest of the space was furnished with second-hand tables, chairs and an old couch, and decorated with AIDS pamphlets, safe sex posters, newspaper clippings about prostitution, and one huge bulletin board that visitors could use to leave messages for one another. No one used the message board, so we papered it with our own announcements. We tried keeping the drop-in open five days and five nights a week but we didn't have enough staff. When we kept long drop-in hours, we had no one doing street outreach, so we cut back on daytime openings and made it a night-time operation.

I enjoyed sitting around talking with people over coffee and cigarettes and I was much better organized than my out-reach co-workers, so I became the mother hen of Maggie's drop-in. A shift began around ten in the evening when I put the coffee on and opened the door. Another staffer showed up around eleven. If no one came by, an entire four- to six-hour shift could pass in a boring haze of cigarette smoke and idle conversation, but most nights had more to offer. Plenty of passersby assumed the drop-in was a coffee shop. (Cabbagetown didn't have a late-night coffee shop in the early nineties — if we had tarted the place up a bit and sold yuppie coffees, we probably could have made a killing.) A large back-lit black and red sign announced our presence, but all it said was "Maggie's." There was no mention of any kind of sex work on the sign, nothing about AIDS, nothing indicating the place was a drop-in. Occasionally someone would huff and puff up the flight of stairs, wander in and ask to see a menu. When we explained that Maggie's was a drop-in for prostitutes, they giggled or made a wisecrack, then left. The hookers and street people who wandered in, all veterans of drop-ins, hostels and shelters, immediately recognized the place for what it was and either picked up a handful of stuff and left or settled in and relaxed.

Like any coffee shop we had our regulars. Sandy, a tiny, tousle-haired heroin addict, always came looking for needles. She hooked in the area whenever she needed money and her addiction, coupled with the high cost of living in Toronto, made her need constant. Sandy was no more than five feet tall and looked like an Auschwitz inmate. In the warmer months she dressed like a little girl — a small pastel T-shirt, shorts, white Reeboks; from a distance, or in the dark, she looked sixteen. The first time I saw Sandy's face in proper lighting I immediately knew she was at least twice that age. When Sandy wasn't high, she was scrappy and bitter, always in a bad mood, but when she was high, she was calm, jovial and easy to deal with. Either way, she only came to Maggie's when she needed needles and she only needed those when she had heroin. When Sandy visited the drop-in straight she always wanted to use our bathroom right after getting her fits. She wasn't interested in coffee or conversation, only in using the toilet. We refused her time and again; we couldn't knowingly allow someone to use the drop-in as a shooting gallery. She would storm out of the place in a huff, shouting curses in her cigarette-scarred voice, only to return about half an hour later, a quieter, gentler person. Often she gave us the used needle so we could get rid of it properly rather than just tossing it in someone's yard.

Mr. D. was a welfare recipient who lived across the street in North Regent Park. He was a fixture in the neighbourhood and a sort of mascot for Maggie's, praising the organization wherever he went. He wasn't a prostitute or a drug user; in fact he hated drugs and their dealers and blamed them for most of Cabbagetown's ills. Mr. D. did like prostitutes and came to Maggie's night after night to be with his favourite women. D. had problems of his own; some nights he was male, other nights female. On her feminine nights Ms. D. came in wearing a rag-tag outfit comprised of clothes given to her by working-girl buddies and items picked up at a local thrift store. Ms. D. acted exactly the same as Mr. D. and often even forgot to shave, but she insisted on being referred to as female. When Mr. D. was himself, he was masculine in every sense of the word. Strange as they may have been, both D.s were friendly and they got along for the most part with Maggie's other regulars.

But we weren't there to provide opportunities for lonely guys to meet prostitutes, even if their intentions were honourable. Sandy and others like her knew why we were in business and they used our services whenever they needed them. She was a street prostitute, as were most of the whores who visited the drop-in. When Maggie's was established, we hoped it would attract street hookers from all over Toronto, and we also hoped indoor workers would occasionally drop by. But indoor workers rarely set foot in the place and their reasons for staying away were as varied as the customers they saw. Some didn't think we had anything to offer them; they knew their AIDS drill, had condoms, didn't use drugs, and weren't looking for information. They had no need of a social service organization and were not interested in getting involved in the fight for prostitutes' rights. There was no reason for these women to come near Maggie's so they didn't. Closeted call-girls stayed away because they didn't want to pick up the whore stigma.

There was nothing we could do to alleviate these fears, and our attempts only played into them. Maggie's sign didn't use words like prostitute, sex industry, sex worker, AIDS or anything that might scare off the closeted. Even the thousands of matchbooks we distributed as advertising for the drop-in excluded these words and neglected to say what we were about. Maggie's was so good at maintaining a low profile that I suspect most of Toronto's prostitutes never heard of us. I wanted the organization to be more open, more public about what we did, but my ideas for increasing our profile were constantly vetoed. Those who opposed increased exposure insisted they were taking their stance for the good of the women. It was not unusual for a Regent Park hooker to wander into the drop-in at midnight on an unforgiving winter's night and ask, "So, what is this place? ... Oh, how long have you been here?" I never understood how Maggie's could benefit prostitutes when so many didn't even know we existed.

Many prostitutes stayed away from Maggie's because they didn't *believe* they were prostitutes. I've seen this attitude on tabloid TV talk shows. A typical show opens with a number of women seated on a stage; half are dressed in tacky, revealing clothing, one or two are obvious drug users. These women are the street prostitutes rounded up from a nearby stroll. The other half of the group is made up of women dressed in better quality, but usually just as revealing, clothing — skimpy cocktail dresses are popular. A couple of these women sport bad wigs and silly sunglasses. These are the high-priced call-girls, some of who claim to be housewives, students or corporate executives by day. The call-girls distance themselves from their sleazy, drugged-out sisters by saying, "We're not prostitutes. Those women are prostitutes. We are escorts, we only cater to gentlemen."

These phoney distinctions exist within the minds of many working in the Business and Maggie's was rarely able to break them down. Whenever a dominatrix's dungeon is raided by the police and she gets slapped with the usual package of bawdy house offences, the first thing she cries is, "I'm not a prostitute. I don't have sex with my clients, I don't even touch them." Maybe her clients just ran around on all fours acting like dogs and perhaps the only thing that caressed them was a cat-o'-nine-tails, but it's still sex (anyone who says otherwise is either a liar or an idiot) and they pay for it. Under Canada's Criminal Code the doms, erotic masseuses and escorts who only cater to gentlemen are prostitutes, whether they like it or not.

Gwendolyn did outreach to a handful of the city's forty-odd strip clubs, but she was rarely welcome in any of them. Club owners believed only prostitutes needed the kind of information Gwendolyn was passing out and if an owner thinks a dancer is tricking in his club he will likely send the woman down the road faster than a drunken customer with no money. The police shut down clubs which double as brothels and club owners know it's easier to lose a liquor licence than it is to get one. Strip clubs make all their money through the sale of liquor and food; dancers are only used as lures to get the customers into the establishments to drink. Whenever Gwendolyn walked into a club and handed out condoms and AIDS pamphlets to strippers, she was putting their jobs at risk. The women who most resented Gwendolyn's presence were the dancers who actually *were* doubling as prostitutes. She brought heat with her, in the form of scrutiny by club owners, which the pros didn't need. Gwendolyn, Danny Cockerline and Chris Bearchell insisted that prostitutes, strippers, even porn performers all share the same problems and Maggie's should treat them all as one — give them condoms and the AIDS rap, encourage them to get involved with the organization, give them jobs. Valerie Scott and I disagreed with the idea of combining everyone who worked in the sex trade under one banner. We didn't believe this made everyone stronger, or that it even made sense. Strippers aren't whores. They may share a similar bad-girl stigma, but other than that, their issues are very different from those of prostitutes. Dancers said they were in the business of selling sexual fantasies, not sex, and they didn't appreciate being lumped together with hookers.

Meanwhile, another battle was being fought over the relationship between Maggie's and its mother group, the Canadian Organization for the Rights of Prostitutes. Cockerline, Bearchell and Gwendolyn considered them one and the same;

Scott, Hotchkiss and I saw them as different entities — Maggie's being a social service organization, CORP a political lobby group. When most other community groups were striving to be more inclusive, we wanted to ensure that CORP remained a prostitutes' organization and that pros had a political voice.

By the summer of 1991 Maggie's had become a potpourri of political arguments and conflicting personalities. The wisest of the new people who got involved tried to distance themselves from the turmoil but inevitably everyone got sucked into one camp or another. When Chris and Danny got involved in the movement they saw themselves as fighting for the rights of those involved in a *lifestyle*, just as they did when they were involved in gay rights. This attitude, adopted by sexual freedom fighters the world over, perpetuates the belief that "once a whore always a whore," and is doomed to failure. Prostitution is a job and the prostitutes' rights movement is about securing the rights of people, primarily women, to work at this job in the manner they choose without fear of harassment — legal or otherwise. Most prostitutes don't buy the prostitution as lifestyle argument, so when Maggie's made it clear that this was what they stood for, the organization alienated itself from the very people it was supposed to help.

My problems with Maggie's ended in January 1992. Since the drop-in first opened, we had hosted an annual Christmas party and 1991 was no exception. All prostitutes were welcomed to the event; drugs and booze weren't allowed but there was plenty of food. However, this was the first party at which there was to be no smoking. If there is a substance prostitutes abuse it's tobacco and every pro I've ever met smoked. Maggie's brand new non-smoking policy was voted in by a majority of the staff but the rule infuriated many of the local pros. One woman called me in the early part of the evening to see if the party was on and to see if the no-smoking rule was being enforced. When I answered yes to both questions, she immediately became upset and vowed to come down and straighten everything out. An hour later she showed up at the drop-in dressed in a short, tight blue dress and heels, her standard work outfit, and reeking of cheap vodka. After greeting a few friends while ignoring most of Maggie's employees, she walked over to a No Smoking sign, ripped it off the wall and set it on fire. Helen, one of the staff members acting as hosts for the party, doused the burning sign and took the woman into the washroom for a little chat. Helen made it clear to the guest that she wasn't going to tolerate any foolishness. She agreed to behave herself; she may even have apologized.

The rest of the party was uneventful enough to be considered boring. But I was fired. The entire melodramatic scene was deemed my fault. I was accused of putting the staff in danger by getting the woman all pumped up over the no-smoking rule then inviting her to the party, knowing she was drunk. Putting another staff member in jeopardy was grounds for dismissal and an emergency board meeting was called early in the new year. Although Helen said she never felt endangered and had no problem convincing the woman to settle down, I wasn't given an opportunity to defend myself. Whenever I spoke up on my own behalf I was interrupted, cut off or shouted down.

The undisputed highlight of my career as a prostitutes' rights activist was attending the Eighth International Conference on AIDS in Amsterdam with Karen in the summer of 1992. We were served the best of two worlds on a silver platter. Karen and I co-authored and presented a paper which criticized the medical and social service professions for treating the private sex lives of prostitutes differently from those of other people. People like Karen, for example, were referred to in a number of studies as "non-paying sex partners of prostitutes." Our paper argued that this practice was discriminatory, and that the private sex lives of prostitutes had to be treated in the same way as everyone else's; otherwise pros and their partners would ignore safe-sex messages directed at them. We had the opportunity to send our message to the top CEOs of the AIDS business, while at the same time seeing what people the world over were saying and doing about prostitution and STDs. We were also drawn by the city itself, famous for its beauty and tolerance.

When I moved from Sudbury to Toronto I thought I was leaving a gulag and entering paradise. A week in Amsterdam revealed just how plastic that paradise was. Amsterdammers don't fear their city, they use it; at four in the morning the narrow cobblestone streets of Centrum, the old city, were filled with revellers, tourists and people just out wandering around — not cars. Restaurants, pubs and shops offer real service and appreciation. Prostitution is evident in much of Centrum; street prostitutes work alongside patio bars; many of the legendary windows are located very near to businesses that have no connection with the sex trade. We watched groups of vacationing families wander through the red-light district every evening and the kids were never as interested in the goings-on as their parents. No one suffered as a result of seeing a lingerie-clad woman sitting in a window seat. The Netherlands is well known, and has often been criticized for, its liberal approaches to drug use, and we didn't see any signs of the War On Drugs in Amsterdam. We also didn't see a city in chaos because people could buy marijuana in a smoking bar and use it without fear of arrest. The feeling of tolerance went far beyond the apparent acceptance of visible prostitution and drug use. We had difficulty spotting class distinctions and saw few power suits on the street. A Dutch bartender summed it up for us, "We respect people here and no one goes out of their way to bother someone else. Amsterdam, unlike North American cities, is a really difficult city to get killed in."

The AIDS conference was an international event and the mood on site varied, depending upon where you were and what you did. The big plenaries, where the medical monarchy of the AIDS business revealed their latest theories, were stuffy, boring affairs highlighted by slide shows and outbursts from community activists. Smaller workshops were cozier, less structured and more useful, but it was impossible to take in all the good ones. When we toured the booths, we were showered with expensive freebies (Cross pens, designer bags), courtesy of the international pharmaceutical companies — or we could smoke grass with the Dutch whores working The Red Thread's display. Our work was well received by representatives from the World Health Organization and many other national and international groups.

We met the delegates from several other prostitutes' rights organizations. COYOTE sent a handful of people who played up their image as sexual freedom fighters. They did not talk about prostitution as work but instead argued for the liberation of the sexually oppressed — bafflegab to most of the working whores I've met. The organizations from Europe and the developing nations often discussed prostitution as work and a pattern quickly developed: the poorer the delegates' home country (and the poorer the delegate) the more she saw prostitution issues as labour issues. Whether prostitution laws contributed to the oppression of people's sexuality was irrelevant to women from South East Asia or South America, where prostitutes are sent to labour camps or executed for trying to earn a living.

Karen and I got along well with the Dutch prostitutes we met, and spent a lot of time talking with them about their work. They told us that the Biz in the Netherlands was far from perfect: licensed brothels were owned by absentee landlords and the women working in them had little say in how they were run; women from developing nations were being brought in to the brothels because they'd work for smaller percentages; prostitutes from eastern Europe were flooding into the Netherlands, looking to make quick money; the rent for the famous windows was too high (about $120 Canadian for eight hours). Despite these problems Dutch prostitutes could still earn decent livings by working on their own, and they faced fewer legal or social hassles than prostitutes in Canada. There was no question that the Dutch pros considered prostitution a job, and apparently so did most Dutch non-prostitute men and women.

On the day following the end of the conference The Red Thread hosted a meeting of the delegates from all the AIDS-related prostitute organizations. Karen and I attended the conference as individuals, but we were also invited to this meeting because of our backgrounds and the paper we had presented. Once everyone arrived, the meeting quickly turned into a planning session as the other delegates devised strategies for defending the prostitution lifestyle. In an adjoining room Karen and I and Margot Alvarez — an old Dutch whore who had worked long enough to raise and house a family — rolled our eyes and drank Heineken out of cans. "Let them be," Margot said, sensing my disappointment in the meeting, "They're just kids, let them do what they want. When they get older they'll learn."

NIMBY!

Like so many mobs, this one moved at night. A heavy June rain washed away all of its tracks, if street shoes and sneakers could leave tracks on concrete. The downpour could not cool the mood of the mob, an angry, violent thing fuelled and fired by chants and placards telling the evil to GET OUT! Parents with children, homeowners, police officers, the mob numbered three hundred and its members had a common mission — drive the evil out. Young men attacked women on the street while the police escorting the crowd did nothing. Bottles were hurled through the windows of homes belonging to other women and still the police did nothing. Journalists and camera crews watched and filmed. The men who beat the women later descended upon an apartment, broke in and trashed the place. The police continued to watch, the cameras continued to roll. The next day a newspaper ran a colour photograph of a woman lying on the street as a group of men punched and kicked her. The vigilantes were denounced and the violence condemned, but the mob's mission was held up as virtuous. The end justifies the means.

This violence didn't occur in a tumultuous developing country. The evil was not a racial or ethnic minority, a contrary political philosophy or an out-of-favour set of religious beliefs. The mob decided to enforce its perceived right to rule in the Montreal neighbourhood of Hochelaga–Maisonneuve and the big evil was the drug trade. In 1993, residents of the area became concerned, and angry, when they found the tell-tale signs of street drug use in their neighbourhood — discarded syringes left in parks and yards during the night. The residents circulated a petition saying they found this intolerable; in a few days thousands of signatures were collected. The petition was given to the police, who said their hands were tied and did nothing. So the citizens of Hochelaga–Maisonneuve took the matter into their own hands and into the streets, with the police providing escort.

Drug dealers and their customers can be an elusive lot and the disgruntled residents needed a focus for their anger, which they found in the neighbourhood's sex trade. Parents marched with kids and kids carried signs saying things like, "Down With Hookers"; "Get Lost"; "Take Your Condoms and Syringes With You"; "Extradite the Sluts." The crowd's chants were far more blunt. The citizens were determined to drive the whores, drug dealers and "shooting galleries" (places were people go to inject heroin) out of the area and they were prepared to use every means at their disposal. They chose to use the most brutal means — intimidation and violence.

Parents felt they had to protect their children. There were stories that prostitutes were offering to masturbate children for a couple of bucks, people were having sex in the streets, drugs were sold in schoolyards, users were everywhere, yards were being littered with condoms. These claims sounded as if they had been pulled straight out of a residents' group anti-prostitution activism kit.

The women beaten on the street were hookers — they may or may not have been drug users. According to a study conducted in the early nineties by Concordia University Professor Fran Shaver, only seven per cent of prostitutes are drug users but it is unlikely the mob considered the numbers when its members attacked the women. The buildings that were pelted with bottles were believed to house prostitutes and the apartment that was destroyed was suspected to be a shooting gallery. Believed, suspected: hardly viable motives for violence and mayhem.

What happened in Montreal in June 1993 is an example of NIMBYism at its worst. The extreme level of violence is rare but the mission — the desire to drive an activity such as prostitution out of a neighbourhood and to hell with grappling with any of the underlying problems — is as common as a downtown stroll. NIMBYism requires three essential elements: a problem (real or perceived, it makes no difference); a cause of the problem (a scapegoat will do, and usually does); and an individual or organization to whip up a neighbourhood and convince its residents to do something about it. The result is to force the cause of the problem (or the scapegoat) out of the area.

Unlike the hookers who were beaten up in Montreal, I didn't have to deal with NIMBYism on a personal level.

However, during my four-year term as a prostitutes' rights activist I was confronted by some form of NIMBYism every summer. My last hurrah as a CORP representative involved wading into the battle that brewed up in Toronto's South Parkdale during the summer of 1992 between residents and street prostitutes. Parkdale's Queen Street West, between Dufferin and Roncesvalles, has been a stroll for as long as most local residents can remember. Infamous for its group homes, psychiatric outpatients, hookers and the drug trade, this area has been known as an inexpensive place to live since the 1970s. Like so many other neighbourhoods in Toronto where street prostitution occurs, it is populated mainly by tenants. Only ten per cent of Parkdale residents are property owners.

Conflicts between residents and prostitutes had been going on for years in Parkdale but all of the previous attempts to drive the hookers out had failed. In the summer of 1992 a new citizens' group sprang up — Residents Against Street Prostitution in Parkdale, or RASPP — and its members began picketing street corners along Queen Street West in an effort to discourage customers from cruising the area. RASPP spokesperson Jane Doesent (her own alias) told the press, "Our children are seeing sex acts, they're picking up needles, hookers aren't allowing us past the corners — and we live here!" Other residents said they did not want to have to explain prostitution to their children; a few admitted they just didn't like prostitutes. Doesent had identified a few problems — public sex, the drug trade, unsafe streets — and successfully linked them to prostitution. As a spokesperson for an anti-prostitution protest group, she was ideally positioned to whip up Parkdale's residents and encourage them

to get involved in RASPP activities. Initially she appeared successful and boasted that RASPP's mailing list included five
hundred names.

Parkdale's pros resisted the pressure put on them by the
residents' group. They said their business wasn't being
affected but they did say the mood in the west end was
getting tense. Some women were afraid that the situation
could get violent, others said it already had. I was well
known as a CORP spokesperson and was asked by a Parkdale
hooker to meet with the women to talk about ways they
could counter RASPP's activities. I agreed and Karen and I
arranged to be in a Parkdale doughnut shop on the night of
September third. We distributed flyers in the west end a few
days beforehand in order to notify the local working women
about the meeting. We also asked Ray Kuszelewski, a
friendly lawyer from a Parkdale Community Legal Services,
to join us — we didn't know what to expect.

When we arrived at the doughnut shop, we ran headlong
into the press, and before any of us had a chance to talk with
the prostitutes, we were interviewed by reporters from *The
Toronto Star, The Globe and Mail* and *The Toronto Sun.*
Mobile units from a couple of local TV stations lurked
outside, the crews hoping to interview one or more hookers.
The women came singly or in pairs and ignored the media,
but they did talk with us. They spoke about being surrounded by residents while standing on street corners trying
to pull dates, or being followed around by groups of
Guardian Angels, an organized vigilante group that had been
active in Parkdale for the last couple of years. One woman
told us that a friend of hers, another prostitute, had been
beaten by the Angels and hospitalized, but her friend wasn't

there to confirm or deny the story. All of the women we spoke with looked tired and haggard — a few spoke in the staccato manner of a person afraid. The legal clinic wanted to document any violence associated with the residents' campaign or the Guardian Angels and we encouraged the dozen or so women we spoke with to cooperate by reporting acts of violence and intimidation. The clinic's lawyer suggested the prostitutes could possibly take legal action against the residents, who may have committed criminal offences by intimidating the women. We agreed to publicly challenge the claims made by RASPP by beginning a media campaign of our own. As well, we agreed to try to drum up more support for Parkdale's pros.

It's impossible for me to say whether this meeting had a direct effect on the situation in Parkdale. No prostitute came forward to the legal clinic in order to lay charges against a member of RASPP. No Guardian Angel was charged with assaulting a prostitute. As the summer cooled into fall the residents stepped up their campaign. RASPP threatened to send suspected clients "Dear John" letters asking the recipients not to visit Parkdale. RASPP placards announced to prospective clients "We Video Johns" but the customers had nothing to fear from this threat. A video camera can intimidate a prospective client but a videotape showing a woman leaning into a car window is not proof that either the woman or anyone in the car is committing a criminal offence. By the end of September the residents' groups (RASPP was being supported by the Parkdale Affirmative Action Committee, PAAC) were claiming at least a partial victory, insisting that their efforts had reduced the number of hookers in Parkdale. *The Toronto Sun* ran a photo of Parkdale resident Arline Smith (formerly known as Jane Doesent) holding up a syringe she claimed to have found in her neighbourhood. Long-time heroin addicts told me the photo had to have been posed because the fit didn't look used. As the weather grew colder, the number of prostitutes working in South Parkdale stabilized at about a dozen on a busy night, essentially the same as in previous years. The picketing residents withdrew into warm houses. The alleged evil is tough and, as the Parkdale experience shows, resilient.

The anti-prostitution activists in Parkdale, like those across the country, said they were taking back their neighbourhood — as if the prostitutes had come into the area and snatched it away from unfortunate homeowners. In fact, the prostitutes had been in Parkdale for a long time (at least since 1965) and most of the pros lived as well as worked in the area. On the other hand many of the most vocal residents were newcomers to the neighbourhood. Arline Smith for instance, the voice of RASPP, purchased her Parkdale home in 1991. Did she and others like her buy houses in Parkdale because the properties were cheap, then get involved in anti-prostitution activism in the hope that by cleaning up the streets their newly purchased properties would increase in value? Property owners new to Parkdale must have known the kind of neighbourhood they were buying into. Parkdale Community Legal Services lawyer Ray Kuszelewski pointed out that the protesting residents didn't constitute a community-wide movement. He described the members of groups like RASPP as a vocal minority involved in resisting many things — group homes, drug rehab centres and other social programs. This small group of residents felt Parkdale already had too many social programs and Kuszelewski believed Smith and her fellow protestors did what they did to enhance the value of their personal property.

Prostitutes are often blamed for a decline in property values. Not long ago I asked a Toronto real-estate agent if Karen and I could get a good deal on a house if we bought one near a stroll. After he stopped laughing, he explained that property values aren't affected by the presence or absence of visible street prostitution but by factors like market activity, the presence or absence of employment and services, and the general state of the economy. He went on to say that if all the local hookers worked in front of the same house, the value of that property might go down but other property values in the neighbourhood wouldn't be affected. When I spoke with a representative of the Toronto Real Estate Board, a body which monitors trends in the industry, he told me the same thing, but instead of laughing at my scheme to buy a house cheaply, he quoted me statistics to disprove the theory that a handful of hookers can lower property values in a given neighbourhood. Realtors have known this for years, yet prostitutes regularly get blamed for falling property values and the resulting decline of neighbourhoods. When the economy nosedives and the bottom falls out of the real-estate market, disgruntled home owners blame the local whores for the devaluation of their properties. Politicians, the police, business people and everyone else looking to court the favour of the angry residents jump on the whore-bashing bandwagon. Prostitutes make great scapegoats, they have no friends in high places and they seldom speak out when saddled with unwanted responsibilities.

Local city councillor Chris Korwin-Kuczynski didn't buy the property-values theory. He claimed that the activism was about family values not property values, but Korwin-Kuczynski has a history of flip-flopping on prostitution-related issues. In 1984 he tried the "hooker patrol" approach to prostitution in his Parkdale ward. The six-foot-six councillor hoped to curb business simply by putting on a red and white sweatshirt with the words "Hooker Patrol" emblazoned on the front and going out and standing near working prostitutes. His strategy didn't work. Then he offered to help find jobs for the working women but he had no takers. In 1986 Korwin-Kuczynski had tried pressuring Attorney-General Ian Scott to ensure that the prostitution laws were upheld in court. "I'm getting fed up, I want these girls out of my area," he said at the time. Still frustrated, in 1988 and again in 1989, the Parkdale politician called for the establishment of red-light districts in Toronto. When no one listened, K.K.K. (as he's known on the street) called for tougher anti-prostitution laws and stiff penalties in order to "wipe the problem from the city's streets." His get-tough plan didn't happen either.

Ed Bozzo, a member of PAAC claimed the actions of his group and RASPP brought members of the community, residents and business owners closer together. He may have been right; people have often united in their opposition to a common enemy. Bozzo said the residents weren't opposed to prostitution in general, just street prostitution, which he insisted was tied to the drug trade. Bozzo also blamed street prostitutes for the spread of AIDS and other sexually transmitted diseases, and claimed they had no morals or ethics. Bozzo's frankness was surprising. Spokespeople for residents' groups usually choose their words more carefully when they talk openly about prostitution. It has become commonplace for the media and many social service agencies to depict prostitutes as victims — of economic circumstance, drug addiction or abusive pimps — and residents' associations don't want to appear as though they're adding to the victimization. Publicly, these groups usually insist that they have nothing personal against the working women, are concerned about their safety, and don't have a moral problem with prostitution, but (and this is the big but) "we just don't want the girls working on our streets" (so we'll push them off and they can go work on your streets). These made-for-the-media comments are lies or, at best, half-truths. The "I'm going to try and make your life hell whenever I'm near you, but I have nothing against you" claim doesn't make sense.

"They're not really cutting into our business, they're just making it more dangerous," said one Parkdale pro during the 1992 turf battle. "We used to stand together and watch each other's backs. Now we're spending more time alone."

Michelle, a thirty-year-old Parkdale prostitute and mother of five school-aged children, told a reporter covering the confrontation, "I was raped by a guy. He took me to his house, beat me, raped me and then said, 'Nobody wants you in this neighbourhood so I can do this to you.'"

A prostitute named Karen was punched in the face; a cut on the bridge of her nose was indicative of the increase in violence on the Parkdale stroll since RASPP began its campaign.

In an interview with Toronto's *eye Weekly* Bozzo stated that the ultimate goal of PAAC "is a higher level of safety, comfort and quality of life in Parkdale." PAAC's vision didn't apply to those residents who worked as prostitutes. He went on to say that Parkdale is "a neighbourhood worth preserving, worth fighting for, and that's what we're here for." If

PAAC and RASPP really believed it was worth preserving, why did they try for two years (1992 and 1993) to change it?

Around the same time, people living in the Jarvis-Maitland area of Toronto's gay village also began actively opposing street prostitution. This area had become known for its transvestite and transsexual pros. A series of meetings was held involving the police, residents, business people and prostitutes' rights activists. Community organizers said the prostitutes who worked the streets in question were also invited but didn't show up. Maggie's, which has always had ties to the gay community, did. While Maitland homeowners complained about noise, litter and traffic volumes, representatives from CORP and Maggie's stressed the importance of dealing directly with the offending nuisances. We suggested that the police ticket litter bugs, arrest drunks and take action against rowdyism. I thought Maggie's would prevail and convince the residents and police to concentrate on the noise and litter instead of casting a wider net over the area's prostitutes. I was wrong. The residents who wanted a police crack-down won out and a year later the cops stepped up their sweeps of the area. This get-tough response drove the pros off Maitland and onto nearby Homewood Avenue.

In the spring of 1993 residents in Toronto's Leaside neighbourhood forced an escort service to shut down. The escort service was breaking a city zoning by-law by operating in a residential area but this contravention was the least of the residents' worries. Ratepayers in the area complained about the noise coming from the house and the cars parked on the street at night. One Leaside resident told *The Toronto Star* she was upset simply because the business was an escort service. She was quoted as saying, "It's on a street with a public school just down the corner." The business was forced out because it was perceived as a threat to the neighbourhood.

Homewood Avenue, a sleepy residential street which parallels Jarvis Street, goes nowhere. The north end of Homewood is capped by the Wellesley Hospital and Wellesley Street, an artery running through Toronto's gay village. The south end stops at Carlton Street and Allan Gardens, a downtown park known as a hangout for drug buyers and sellers, and as a place where gay men have sex under the stars. The west side of Homewood is made up of two condominium towers and a couple of low-rise apartment buildings. Two old houses remain standing on the north end, stubborn survivors of the wrecking ball and Toronto's urge to build up. The east side of the street still boasts a collection of houses, some quite attractive, some not. Many of these buildings have been converted into rooming houses or subdivided into apartments; the tenant population is varied. The upper half of the street is tree-lined but the trees peter out as Homewood reaches down to Carlton. After dark a dozen old pole lamps illuminate the street, making nighttime Homewood pretty but potentially dangerous. After the sun sets, Homewood Avenue is a fine place in downtown Toronto to commit double murder.

I lived on the twenty-seventh floor of 40 Homewood from the spring of 1990 to the summer of 1991. My small apartment, with its panoramic view of the Jarvis Street stroll, was a workplace and a home. I saw many customers there and if any of the other tenants figured out what I was doing they never said so. While I lived there I never heard my neighbours complain about any kind of prostitution, not even the street trade that occurred down the street on Carlton. Hookers who worked the Homewood/Carlton corner liked the location because few people bothered them. The whores, in turn, didn't bother the residents. The police did occasionally sweep the area but generally the business environment was low key, almost subdued. Within two years all this changed.

Homewood's residents didn't want prostitutes soliciting on their street but they didn't simply demand that the police crack down on prostitution in the area. Perhaps the residents realized that the simple get-tough approach to street prostitution had never worked in Toronto. A residents' association held a series of community meetings with local politicians, police and prostitutes to discuss their concerns and to map out a course of action which could bring results acceptable to all the players. In 1995 the residents association sent a letter to Justice Minister Allan Rock, calling for the decriminalization of voluntary, adult prostitution. This was an unusual move for a Toronto-based residents' group, but the letter had no effect on the government. Rock wasn't interested in looking at more liberal approaches to prostitution and whenever he spoke publicly about the business he always talked about harsher laws and penalties — the same old line. The liberal-minded Homewood residents learned they couldn't teach newly elected politicians new tricks.

On Victoria Day 1996, prostitutes Shawn Keegan and Deanna Wilkinson were found shot to death on Homewood Avenue. They were killed by the same gun, likely fired by the same shooter during the holiday's fireworks displays — the explosions of the fireworks masking the discharges of the weapon. The bodies were discovered a mere stone's throw from one another. The Homewood Avenue residents' association quickly showed another side of itself and blamed the prostitutes working the street for bringing violence into a previously safe neighbourhood. Much of the local media willingly participated in this "blame the victim" response to the murders. The Homewood neighbourhood was described as being a zoo at night and one Toronto columnist referred to the prostitutes as "creatures." Reporters seemed to delight in repeatedly telling their readers that Keegan was dressed as a woman when he was killed, and constantly referring to Wilkinson, a male-to-female transsexual, as "he." The murdered whores became freaks and the frightened residents became active.

Evening walks were organized by the Homewood residents, and flyers were distributed to nearby apartment buildings inviting the tenants to join the Homewood residents in their efforts to drive the hookers off their street. No mention was made on the flyers of making the streets safe for all people — the plan was simply to drive the hookers out. During the investigation of the Victoria Day shootings the press had a field day. Within two weeks *The Toronto Sun* and *The Star* published over fifty stories on prostitution and the murders, while television news programs turned prostitution into a staple. During one broadcast an elderly man approached councillor Kyle Rae (Homewood Avenue is in Rae's ward) and told him it was too bad that the shooter didn't have more bullets in his gun. "It's one way to get rid of the hookers," the old man told the councillor. Rae believes the man was a Homewood Avenue resident.

The murders of Keegan, Wilkinson and Brenda Ludgate (a prostitute found murdered in Parkdale, shot with the same gun that killed Keegan and Wilkinson) didn't only galvanize the residents of a downtown Toronto neighbourhood in their war on prostitution, they also gave a couple of Metro councillors an opportunity to grab some limelight. Councillor Judy Sgro's personal campaign against prostitution began in 1994, after she failed to get rid of five prostitutes working in her North York ward. She raised a fuss and the Metro Police Services Board responded by creating an anti-prostitution task force and appointing her and fellow councillor Brian Ashton co-chairs. In 1995 Sgro created a Toronto version of San Francisco's John School and waited for the randy tricks to graduate as good, clean husbands and fathers. This was a rehash of an old theory: curb the demand and kill the business.

After the Victoria Day murders Sgro told *The Toronto Sun* that at least one hundred of Toronto's street prostitutes were HIV positive and described the women as "walking time bombs." Near the end of May the task force held a public meeting on prostitution in the City of York. Being a freelance journalist working on a story about the outspoken Sgro, I attended the meeting. The gathering was held in a school auditorium and by the time I arrived the room was packed with locals and representatives of residents' groups from all over the city. Sgro served as mistress of ceremonies for this anti-prostitution pep rally. Most of the evening was turned over to politicians and police officers who praised their own efforts while condemning street prostitution. No one spoke about the three murders which had occurred only a week ago. No one talked about making Toronto's streets safer for everyone. Instead, the audience applauded tales of john stings, raids on crack houses, and other examples of the flexing of police muscle. The evening was topped off by former Liberal MP John Nunziata, who took the podium with Sgro and condemned the ruling Liberal government for being too soft on prostitution. The audience loved it all.

Valerie Scott from CORP was present. She called for the decriminalization of prostitution and beseeched the residents to support CORP's position, arguing that prostitutes would leave the streets if they could legally work out of their homes. She was treated to a chorus of "Get a job," and "Get out of our neighbourhood." The merchants and homeowners in attendance weren't interested in hearing alternative solutions to street prostitution problems, particularly those being pitched by a whore. Kara Gilles, prostitute and employee of Maggie's, supported Scott's argument and added that residents should work with pros' rights organizations in an effort to find equitable short- and long-term solutions. She got the same compassionate response from the audience as did Valerie Scott. As Gilles attempted to answer a question put to her by one resident, Sgro stepped in and told Kara to "sit down and be quiet."

NIMBYism can spread faster than spores on the wind. When one neighbourhood decides to confront street prostitution, others often follow suit. Prostitutes driven out of one area just go to another and the process begins anew. Groups like CORP and Maggie's have always been composed of only a few people, and even if the organizations had wanted to visibly oppose NIMBYism in Toronto, they lacked the bodies to do so. At times the prevailing mood among CORP and Maggie's was that directly confronting NIMBYism was a waste of time. The residents had made up their minds to harass prostitutes and that was that; no amount of social working or community outreaching was going to change their minds.

In the summer of 1995 Toronto's city council took a courageous step forward and called on the federal government to decriminalize voluntary, adult prostitution. Oddly, Maggie's remained quiet during the debate which led up to council's decision, and afterwards, as various chiefs of police and politicians condemned it. I know the media was hounding Maggie's for comment — I hadn't turned a trick for years but the press was calling me. I refused to say anything; I was working as a freelance journalist and was no longer a prostitute or a CORP member. I've always thought the idea of one journalist interviewing another about an issue, when there are people available who are directly involved, is wrong (and silly). I passed all of my calls onto Maggie's and Valerie Scott of CORP. Council's advocation of decriminalization was just the kind of high-profile endorsement Maggie's needed to back up its own call for change but the organization never seized the moment. Beth Wolgemuth, a Maggie's employee at the time, told me her co-workers were tired of saying the same thing over and over. One of the primary tasks of any community-based group is to continually get its message out. It appears that by 1995 Maggie's had grown tired of this drudgery.

I suspect all of us, at one time or another, have tried to drive something out of our backyards, or at least thought about getting involved in some NIMBY action. I don't want to live next door to a nuclear refinery and I sympathize with people who don't wish to grow twenty-pound peas or see their kids glow in the dark. I'd get mighty upset if my city council said it was okay for Wal Mart to build a concrete shopping haven across the street from my home. Who wants to live downwind from a garbage incinerator or watch their kids play in a toxic-waste dump? I can understand, sympathize with, even get involved in protesting against blights like these. The problems they cause are obvious but the same can't be said about prostitution. And odds are NIMBYism directed against street prostitution won't work, so why do people bother with it at all?

Instead of harassing prostitutes and their clients, ratepayers should lobby the federal government to change our existing prostitution laws to allow women to work indoors, which would get most prostitutes off the streets permanently. If making the streets safer was really the issue, NIMBY-minded activists would think twice before hoisting their placards and hitting the streets. NIMBY activism makes the streets more dangerous for prostitutes by conveying the idea that they are deserving of harassment and perhaps even violence. A man who would rob or assault a prostitute could just as easily do the same to any woman, so when you make the streets unsafe for hookers you make them unsafe for all women.

NIMBYism will not protect children from the potential perils of the urban environment. Prostitutes pose no threat to the school children who see them and I doubt that any prostitute has ever seriously tried to solicit a schoolboy as a customer. Many prostitutes are themselves mothers and there is no reason to assume that one who works as a whore feels any differently about young kids than any other working mother. As for the concern that young children might see sex acts happening in public, those same children see sex on television all the time, as well as a never-ending stream of blood and gore. Which will have a greater impact on kids: seeing a prostitute servicing a client in an alleyway or seeing thousands of televised murders before the age of thirteen? I also question the wisdom of parents who take their kids along on anti-prostitution protests. What do seven-year-olds learn when they're told to carry signs saying things like "Extradite the sluts"? What do they learn when they see adult men beating women on the street? When it comes to NIMBYism, prostitution and children, the attempted cure is likely more dangerous than the perceived disease.

The driving forces behind today's NIMBYism are fear and the desire to create and maintain homogenous neighbourhoods. In 1994, Metro Toronto councillors Tony O'Donohue and Betty Disero put their heads together and dreamed up the ill-fated three's-a-crowd by-law. If passed, this ruling would have made it an offence for three or more people to hang out together on the city's streets or on municipally controlled property such as the Parking Authority's lots. The by-law was defeated in council because the majority of councillors considered it "too facist." Unfortunately this defeat didn't send any sort of message to other local politicians and the silliness continued. The following year Councillor Peter Tabuns tried to ban dancing in his ward after constituents complained about the noise coming from restaurants featuring dancing and live music, and the difficulty they were having finding parking spaces near their homes on the weekends. These people didn't like seeing strange cars in their neighbourhood either. Tabuns suggested the city create specific entertainment zones, special areas in town where people could go to do things like dance or listen to live music. Other areas of this world-class city, such as Councillor Tabuns's ward, were to be designated dance-free zones. Restaurateurs, musicians and people who like to dance objected and Tabuns's proposal died a quick death, but this illustrates just how far some people are willing to go to create their own versions of Sleepy Hollow, and how far some politicians will go to improve their chances of being re-elected.

There are alternatives to the confrontational NIMBY approach to prostitution. Municipal governments could instruct their police forces to selectively enforce our present anti-prostitution laws. The cops could continue sweeping residential areas while not charging pros working on commercial streets. The prostitutes would move to the commercial areas. The police shouldn't bother investigating escort services or individual call-girls at all unless someone complains about a specific service or escort. Complaints of violence and other serious crimes reported by prostitutes should be investigated fully. This approach would make better use of limited police resources. Once the prostitutes learned the new rules of the game the number of prostitution-related arrests would likely go down, thereby reducing the burden on our over-worked court system, and the police and the courts could concentrate more of their efforts on real crime. Selective enforcement has been suggested many times in the past and the police response has traditionally been: We can't do that, we have to enforce the laws as they stand. In fact, police forces regularly practise selective enforcement. For example, a couple of years ago in Toronto the Metro Police Services Board decided it would concentrate its anti-drug efforts on mid- and upper-level dealers instead of going after street dealers and individual drug users. Toronto's cops still arrested street dealers and users but usually only after receiving complaints from affected neighbourhoods.

Residents' associations could improve their neighbourhoods simply by improving their area's physical appearance. Open the boarded-up storefronts. Get rid of offensive graffiti. Clean up the parks. And imaginative thinking should be used whenever possible. Over the years a number of downtown Toronto apartment buildings had problems with drug dealers doing business in stairwells. None of the traditional responses to this problem — new locks on doors, police patrols, increased paid security — successfully curbed the dealers. A couple of buildings began piping classical music into the stairwells, another piped in CBC radio. The dealers and their customers must not have cared much for the likes of Mozart and Peter Gzowski because the amount of dealing occurring in the stairwells of the buildings dropped dramatically. Cheap, simple and effective, not to mention harmless; the idea to pipe in the low-impact music and dull radio was brilliant. Now the Toronto Transit Commission is considering doing the same thing in subway stations known for youth and gang-related violence.

NIMBY actions are, by their very nature, exclusive — agree with us or get out. An activity such as a street festival, on the other hand, conveys a different message (come and join in) and gives everyone an opportunity to get to know each other. NIMBYism doesn't help bring communities together, it fractures them. People living in the affected areas are divided into different camps: those who agree and those who disagree, property owners and tenants, the good citizens and the bad, the haves and the have-nots. The more fractured a community is, the easier it is for real undesirable elements to move in and the more difficult it is for neighbourhoods to deal with them. A unified, inclusive community is the best deterrent to crime and violence. A unified community can only be created after its members begin dealing with each other in an atmosphere of understanding and tolerance.

chapter 11

Red Lanterns, White Picket Fences

One of my responsibilities as a Maggie's employee was to attend the seasonal meetings of the Ontario AIDS Network (OAN). During these meetings delegates from the member organizations exchanged current AIDS information and discussed new ideas and strategies for AIDS prevention. Shop talk was the order of the day but a lot of socializing went on as well and friends had plenty of opportunities to get together. The first OAN meeting I attended was in the spring of 1990, a gathering held in Guelph. Maggie's had been involved with the OAN for a couple of years but I had no idea who was who or what was what. Karen Maki, a delegate from the AIDS Committee of Thunder Bay or ACT-B, took me under her wing. ACT-B is the second-oldest community-based AIDS organization in Ontario (only the AIDS Committee of Toronto is older) and Karen is one of ACT-B's founding members. She took me around and introduced me to everyone, making me feel welcome and part of the group. Karen also filled me in on all the really important details new delegates need: where the coffee and snacks were stashed and where we had to go to catch a smoke.

OAN meetings only last a weekend and I didn't see Karen again until the Canadian AIDS Society met months later in Winnipeg. During this conference we spent a lot of time together and I found Karen to be a warm, sensual woman who could make me laugh. I felt I could be open and honest with her (a rarity in my life) and everything clicked for us; we fell in love and began acting like a couple. We tried living in a long-distance relationship for almost a year. We made a point of attending the same conferences and meetings and she flew to Toronto every chance she got. Everyone in our respective agencies knew what was going on and Karen's boss, Michael Sobota, the executive director of ACT-B, was particularly good about letting her come south as often as possible so we could be together.

Karen had already guessed that I was in transition and she knew what I did for a living. Whenever she flew into town I turned off the answering machine and let the clients wait until I was alone again. I didn't do this because Karen had problems with prostitution. When other people asked her how she felt about my work she always answered, with a straight face, "I'm just glad she has a good job." I always felt so proud hearing her say so. I turned off my machine because I didn't want our short time together interrupted by the work. As a result, we had a few highly emotional conversations about it. Karen was afraid she was taking up too much of my prime working time and somehow compelling me to drift away from prostitution. I explained just how important the breaks from the work were and how much I needed and enjoyed our time together. Besides, my paid work for Maggie's had already allowed me to devote less time to working as a prostitute. I knew Karen understood the differences between commercial and intimate sex, but deep down inside I began to wonder whether I understood the differences myself.

Karen was a staunch advocate of prostitutes' rights and a dedicated ally of both CORP and Maggie's. When asked, she offered her advice and expertise as a first-rate fundraiser to both groups. She advised me, whenever I had to deal with the media, on how to dress and act in front of the camera or on a well-lit stage (checking out the audience while on stage by holding one hand over your eyes is a real no-no). I respected her knowledge and followed her suggestions. While I was a CORP spokesperson I picked and chose my media appearances carefully. I wanted the fifth estate to take me and the organization I represented seriously. I made a point of responding quickly and professionally to the legitimate press, knowing full well that certain media outlets always put either a negative or a sensational spin on prostitution stories. Karen also taught me the value of saying no, and calls from American tabloid talk shows went unanswered unless we were looking for a cheap laugh. The Geraldo Show once offered us limos to and from the airports, airline tickets, a room in a good New York City hotel and one thousand U.S. dollars to appear as guests on the program but we refused. I was never a trashy hooker.

The distance between Thunder Bay and Toronto put a tremendous strain on us and each time we had to say goodbye it became more difficult. When she was gone I wrote long letters, took on enough work to fill up most of my days, and eventually began to dabble with heroin. Heroin seduced me long before I ever poked a vein with a needle. I had read a lot about the drug and listened to junkies and ex-junkies talk about the happiness and horrors brought on by its use. Heroin seemed to be a ten-second ticket to either Heaven or Hell and I wanted to know where it would take *me*. I had used a wide range of drugs off and on since my middle teens and, except for LSD I found most of them boring and over-rated. Acid jangled my senses so that for six or seven hours at a time I could live in a different place, at least one that looked and sounded different from where I was when I was straight — and I liked it. Heroin held the promise of being able to do the same thing. Are we talking about escapism here? — yes, or at the very least vacationism.

I threw up violently the first few times I used heroin but every time the vomiting ended the drug faithfully carried me to any one of a number of places. I called this heroin dreaming and unlike so many of the hallucinogenics I'd taken in the past the dreamscapes were always mysteries until I arrived. As the highs wore off, the dreamscapes were slowly replaced by reality until finally I was sober again. It wasn't long before my body developed enough of a tolerance that I could do a hit without throwing up, and this enabled me to enjoy the rush that comes with injecting. Seconds after hitting heroin, total oblivion roared through my body, leaving me totally vulnerable and in the grip of the junk until the rush ended and heroin dreaming began.

At first I only used a couple of times a month. That soon changed to a couple of times a week and by the end of the summer of 1991, when Karen moved to Toronto, I was using almost once a day. I never saw a client or worked a shift for Maggie's stoned, but heroin did affect my private life. Once I was using fairly regularly, the drug usurped all of my past personal pleasures. I stopped reading, stopped writing, and lost interest in activities I had been keen on for years. I collect and paint fantasy figurines; I find the meticulous work very relaxing and have nearly sixty completed pieces in my collection. I've been told that I have a talent for painting miniatures and have done commission work for other collectors. When I picked up the needle, I put down my brushes. I never lost my interest in Karen though and when she arrived in Toronto to stay, I was the happiest girl in the city, except perhaps for her. During our first night together, I told her about my drug use and invited her to try junk "just one time; we could get high together." Karen would have none of that.

In a voice that invited no compromise, she told me she didn't move to Toronto to live with a junkie. I knew what I had to lose and never used heroin again. My habit was not deeply ingrained so my withdrawal was quite mild; in a couple of weeks my addiction was broken. It wasn't until I began reading, writing and painting again that I realized just how heroin had altered my life. All of these activities felt new and my enthusiasm for them grew in leaps. I have painted the best pieces in my figurine collection since I quit using junk.

People who know something of my past often don't believe that I've always been faithful to Karen. "But you were a prostitute and you continued to work even after you fell in love and got involved with her. Of course you cheated on her, she just accepted it." Wrong! There was no intimacy between my clients and me regardless of what took place in my bedroom or theirs. The clients held no special feelings for me nor did I for them. This dynamic can change — I had feelings for Hal and I believe he did for me; under different circumstances we might have become casual sex partners, but that's pure speculation. The reality is if he hadn't responded to my ad we would never have met. I've rarely found any man sexually attractive regardless of how well he could treat me. Condoms serve as intimacy barriers but so does the money; the men who paid me for sex were always, first and foremost, tricks, and the moment was over the instant their money ran out. This lack of intimacy is crucial to understanding the differences between paid sex and love-making. (I recall two customers — one a wealthy Toronto business man, the other a retired senior — who fell in love with me. They both wanted to save me from prostitution and promised me money, safety and security if only I quit working and moved in with them. Their offers were flattering but acceptance was out of the question.)

Commercial sex lacks intimacy, trust, spontaneity and deep affection, so what's left? — the mechanics, exactly what prostitutes have always said. The sex between prostitute and client is usually even more meaningless than sex between two people having a one-night stand. Everyone involved knows how the commercial act will end even before it begins. There are no strings attached and the strings are what make all the other varieties of sex more complicated, interesting and better. If my having upfront, meaningless mechanical sex with strangers for money weakened a relationship, then the relationship was never very strong in the first place.

While I was working the Biz, Karen and I were often asked what our day-to-day personal life was like, as if prostitution affected every aspect of our lives. I know prostitution is often referred to as a lifestyle, but it's not — it's a job — and, apart from my work, our life together was very ordinary. We kept the Business separate from our personal life as much as we could. We rented a two-bedroom townhouse in downtown Toronto and the second bedroom served as the trick room. We had two phone lines installed in our home, one for business and the other for personal use. Either I or an answering machine always answered the work line and I booked more outcalls than incalls in order to minimize the number of clients who came to the house. When Valerie Scott heard of our arrangement, she scoffed and insisted that every whore's home was first a place of work — a brothel — but we believed she was wrong. Our lifestyle certainly wouldn't interest a supermarket tabloid reporter; we had friends from outside the Business, we shopped for food at our local grocery stores, we had pets, watched the six o'clock news. Our personal life was typical for a lesbian couple living in a large city — mundane to the point of being boring to a voyeur. We were very happy.

There was only one real dark spot in our lives — the gender identity clinic at the Clarke Institute where I had to convince the psychiatrists that I was indeed a woman in transition and not just an enthusiastic cross-dresser or a gay man in denial. I had to do this in order to be recommended for sex reassignment surgery, but the trick was to do it without compromising too much of my own identity. I dealt with four doctors from the Clarke — all shrinks, all men. Women were involved in the process but they performed in a supportive role and more often than not they supported the doctors — the men. Since 1989 I have filled out numerous psychiatric evaluation forms and when these questionnaires delved into sex and personal relationships the focus was on sex with men and relationships with — you guessed it — men. In my naïvety I never thought men would play such a dominant role in determining whether or not I should be treated as a woman.

During face-to-face evaluations I had many heated discussions with members of my "gender team," as they called themselves, and often an evaluation at the Clarke was followed by crying jags at home, but I did make headway. I connected with a good family doctor and he put me on hormone therapy right away, even though the Clarke's psychiatrists initially advised against it. Later they changed their minds and accepted my hormone use provided it was closely monitored by my family physician, which it was. The Clarke's doctors refused to acknowledge prostitution as work because it didn't produce a tax receipt, so I got a job hustling coffee in a Second Cup outlet. Once I got the tax receipt I quit the job, gave the paper to the Clarke and went back to hooking. This proved to the doctors that I could get and keep a traditional female job (like prostitution isn't?) — the kind that pays very low wages and holds little promise for advancement. My relationship with the Clarke improved again when I began doing AIDS-related work and when my writing as a freelance journalist started appearing in the Toronto papers — more proof that I could support myself outside the sex trade.

Once Karen moved to Toronto, the Clarke had to acknowledge my orientation and face the fact that men played a very minor role in my personal life. In the late summer of 1992 we met with staff from the Clarke for a family visit and after this meeting my dealings with the doctors improved dramatically. Karen's candid descriptions of our day-to-day lives showed them that I was being accepted as a woman in the real world, and her very presence in my life validated everything I had been telling the doctors about myself since Day One. In 1993 I was unofficially approved for surgery; all I needed to do was take care of the legal and financial arrangements — the wait was over. I like to think I could have done it all on my own, but I hate to think how hard it would have been.

There are few rules when it comes to the affairs of the human heart. There's no doubt that the whore stigma can affect every aspect of a prostitute's life but that doesn't mean that everyone she meets will believe all the negativity that has grown up around it. People meet and fall in love in myriad situations and for an infinite variety of reasons and I have never met a prostitute who wasn't involved with somebody. Husbands, lovers and children are as common to the prostitute women I know as they are to straight women, and the home lives of many working women — their lives away from the strolls, the agencies or the phones — are quite mundane. The private lives of these women don't revolve around drugs, sex or shady characters who dress in flashy clothes and wear too much jewellery. These women are more concerned about how their kids are doing in school and who they are hanging around with, whether their landlords are going to raise the rent, and the cost of groceries. Many of the younger women who get into the Biz often get caught up in a vortex of money and the fast life but the flush wears off quickly because no one stays a fresh new face for long. Once the glamour wears off, and the harder you work the sooner this happens, the new faces learn that all they've got is a job in the business of prostitution. What they make of it is up to them.

Friendships develop through the work. Street prostitutes often hang out in the same places — bars and coffee shops, street corners — and it's inevitable that the women get to know each other. There's nothing unusual about this and it's common to every line of work. Indoor workers, who tend to be more secretive about how they earn their living, seldom find the same opportunity to get to know their peers. Street prostitutes have to deal with the police, residents' associations and gawkers, but they don't have to deal with the sort of isolation that comes with working indoors. Laura began working as a freelance call-girl in the late 1980s but eventually took up with a small escort agency because she didn't like the feeling of always being alone. "I had no one else in the Business to talk to and no one to watch my back when I went out on a call. I hated it." The agency's owner was a friendly, out-going woman who, surprisingly, encouraged the women in her employ to visit her office and to get to know their co-workers (most owners discourage contact between escorts). Laura met other working women and made lasting friendships with a few.

Economic forecasters spin cautious tales of growth, but the economy in Toronto and the rest of the province is a mess. No one feels secure in their jobs, the social safety net has been blown apart by the provincial and federal governments, the youth unemployment rate is in the double digits. The gap between the haves and the have-nots is widening and the middle class fears it will be wiped out by high taxes and companies that are maximizing their profits by firing everyone who is not absolutely essential. What does this doom and gloom have to do with prostitution? — everything. More people are getting into the Business out of economic necessity and the competition among Toronto's prostitutes has really toughened. The strolls are filling up with new and old faces, the back pages of entertainment tabloids swell with ads, and both venues are going after the same customers. Prices for sex are falling. In Toronto a customer can hire an escort for as little as sixty-five dollars; that used to be a street price and being able to hire an inside working girl for such a low fee was unheard of when I returned to the city in the spring of '89. Employment ads placed by escort services claim the women can earn up to $4,000 weekly. A prostitute working at Toronto's prices would have to turn over a hundred tricks a week, or more than ten a day, to make that kind of money — impossible.

Yet despite all the troubles friendships on the street survive. In the spring of '96 three people thought to be prostitutes were murdered in downtown Toronto. Shock, anger, fear and grief passed quietly over the strolls like soaring vultures as everyone concerned came to grips with what had happened. A local organization, the Sex Workers Alliance of Toronto, held a candlelight vigil for the slain streetwalkers and dozens of hookers participated; many wept openly as they stood in a tight group and clutched their Dixie cup candle holders. Toronto's media lurked in the shadows created by their own floodlights, ready to shove microphones into the faces of anyone willing to talk, and there were a few. They spoke about friendship and loss and the dangers of street work, and why it's necessary for prostitutes to stick togther. Perhaps that's why friendships among prostitutes are often as strong as they are. When the hard times hit, who else can whores turn to; who else can understand the work and its environment?

chapter 12

Is This
the Business
for You?

Bleecker Street is a low-end stroll in Toronto running between Carlton and Wellesley streets, just east of Sherbourne Street. Some say it lies on the eastern fringe of Cabbagetown, others say Bleecker is a part of the "new Cabbagetown" and is not really a part of *Cabbagetown* Cabbagetown, old Cabbagetown, the neighbourhood authors have written about, the neighbourhood that shelters historic homes cherished and enjoyed long before Martha Stewart invited us into hers. At nine on a mid-October morning a black woman dressed in a flimsy green windbreaker and too-short shorts shivers away on the south end of the street. I walk towards her; I'm dressed in no-nonsense winter clothes and she mistakes me for a man.

"You want to go out?" she asks.

Her movements are jerky but she's not high, she's cold. She's wearing cheap running shoes, the kind you buy in the spring, expecting to discard them when the weather turns like it is this morning — cold.

"No, I don't want to go out," I reply. "Say, why are you working out here dressed like that? You'll freeze your butt off. Bad enough you have to worry about picking up dates, dressed like that you could catch cold or something."

She smiles and crosses her arms in front of herself. "I know, but I've got to work; I have to make some money." She hasn't been in the Business long. Bleecker is too quiet at nine in the morning to offer her much chance of breaking. An experienced street whore would know this, would know that Bleecker picks up in the afternoon and evening.

The other afternoon, on the north end of the street at Wellesley: A woman built like a little girl and defying the rain by wearing only summer clothes and Reeboks tries hard to pull a date off the corner. She knows traffic has to stop at the top of Bleecker before turning east or west onto Wellesley and that's when she makes her move, dashing up to the driver's side and talking through the window. She's obviously high, crack probably. Opiate users — junkie whores — don't move that fast. The traffic is heavy; plenty of cars, lots of people. Some of the older pedestrians watch her with disdain, neighbourhood teenagers giggle at her antics. A lone driver refuses her advances.

We are urged to assume all street prostitutes, perhaps all prostitutes, are drug addicts. Journalists interview crack- or heroin-addicted hookers, then tell stories about the links between drugs and prostitution and the horrors of both. We seldom hear about the prostitutes who aren't caught up in addictions and it's easy to reject the notion that someone would sell sex for reasons other than to finance a drug habit.

Although the majority of prostitutes are not drug abusers, there are more pros working essentially for drugs now than when I got into the Biz over twenty years ago, and there are more addicted pros working now than even five years ago. The number of prostitutes is going up while the going rates for sex are dropping and while the increase in the numbers of working women has affected prices, so has the influx of crack-cocaine. When the drug of choice is expensive, even the pros working primarily for their next fix have to make a decent amount of money before they can score. They aren't interested in turning nickle-and-dime tricks, they waste time. We're living in an era of drug prohibition and crack is the era's bathtub gin — cheap, potent and easy to make — and its market is the poor. A heroin high might have cost a user a hundred dollars or more in 1991; today a crack high costs next to nothing and it's sold everywhere. If a desperate crack-addicted prostitute hits the stroll planning to work just long enough to afford her next hit, she may go with a customer for twenty bucks or less. If a handful of crack addicts are working a stroll, the other women may be forced to lower their prices to stay competitive.

The prostitutes' rights movement has, in recent years, veered away from the bread-and-butter issues of the trade. At times CORP and Maggie's form loose relationships with other sex workers (a catch-all phrase which includes whores, strippers and porn performers), regardless of whether their views are popular with prostitutes. Chris Bearchell, Danny Cockerline and Gwendolyn all had strong links to the gay rights movement and to people involved with *The Body Politic*, particularly journalist and prostitute Gerald Hannon.

Hannon became notorious in the late seventies because of an article he wrote which espoused the open discussion of "intergenerational sex" (a euphemism for sex between adults and children). He has since been accused of advocating pedophilia and in 1995 controversy over his views erupted when a Toronto newspaper columnist questioned whether he should be teaching freelance magazine writing to Ryerson University's journalism students. Oddly enough, during an interview with *Toronto Sun* columnist Heather Bird, the fifty-one-year-old journalism instructor disclosed that he moonlights as a prostitute. Hannon's teaching career at Ryerson was endangered and in the summer of 1996 the university's hiring committee decided not to renew his contract. This story has more sides than an old-fashioned nickel, but if you ask a prostitute what she thinks of a grown man having sex with kids, odds are she will respond with disgust. Most prostitutes have no use for adults who promote sex with children. Yet Gerald Hannon was an early board member of Maggie's, which has continued to support him in his struggle for freedom of expression. I think it odd that Maggie's would support someone who holds views that so many working women find repugnant.

When I began hooking in 1972 the laws affecting indoor prostitution were in place, but there was no law specifically addressing street prostitution. The vagrancy or "Vag C" law, which said a woman had to be able to account for her being on the street or risk being prosecuted as a common prostitute, had been used against streetwalkers since the prohibition era but it was abolished in 1972. Vag C's opponents said the focus of a street prostitution law had to be shifted from a status offence (an offence involving no specific behaviour) to one prohibiting soliciting. The new law, Section 195.1 of the Criminal Code, made it an offence to solicit in a public place for the purpose of prostitution and for the next nine years judges in Canada tried to figure out just what the word "solicit" meant. Was a wink or a nod a form of soliciting? How about a casual conversation? Judges were also not too clear on exactly what a public place was. The police argued that if the term didn't include customers' cars (hardly public places in the minds of automobile owners) they would not be able to control street prostitution. In 1978 the Supreme Court ruled that for soliciting to be seen as a crime it had to be pressing or persistent but the action still wasn't given a legal definition. The police reacted by saying their hands were tied by the decision.

By the early eighties many cities virtually stopped enforcing the soliciting law altogether. Accordingly, citizens started raising a fuss over street prostitution, and in June 1983, the federal government created the Special Committee on Pornography and Prostitution (the Fraser Committee) to study prostitution in Canada on behalf of the Ministry of Justice. The Fraser Committee held twenty-two public and private meetings across Canada and found that the street prostitution issue divided the Canadian public. Municipal politicians, the police and residents groups wanted the laws used against street prostitution toughened up, while civil libertarians, women's groups and social service agencies favoured some form of decriminalization.

In May 1985, the committee issued a report which contained sixteen recommendations dealing with adult prostitution. The Fraser Report described prostitution as a social problem requiring both legal and social reforms. The committee saw prostitutes and their customers as willing, responsible participants who shouldn't be doing their thing in public but who had a right to the same protection from violence, threats and coercion that is available to all citizens. The committee stated that the existing anti-street prostitution law was unsatisfactory and suggested it be repealed. The nuisance aspect of street soliciting could be dealt with using laws designed to curtail disorderly conduct. The Fraser Report went on to recommend that the anti-pimping laws be rewritten in order to clearly prohibit violence and threats of violence rather than focusing on the hard-to-define exploitation of prostitutes. The committee also recommended the rewriting of the bawdy-house laws in order to allow small numbers of prostitutes to work from their homes and to allow the provinces to regulate these small-scale brothels.

In short the Fraser Committee, the most detailed look at prostitution ever undertaken in Canada, came out in favour of the partial decriminalization of voluntary adult prostitution and since then every federal government has ignored it.

There are more women working in prostitution now than when the Fraser Committee began studying the Biz over ten years ago. The high-end strolls are still office to women who look like money but the faux fur coats and expensive hooker drag outfits are fewer and farther between. There's plenty of traffic, and circle jerks still cruise the blocks, but the affluent strolls don't have the same feel of fast money they did only five years ago. None of the women are staggering around or jumping out onto the street, but that kind of action is more common on the low-end tracks where drug use is more prevalent and open. A quick flip through the escort pages in the weeklies reveals plenty of ads, but now more and more of them mention the fees — low fees.

It's not illegal to be a hooker in Canada but our prostitution laws have been described as the most draconian in the Western world. Our lawmakers never seem totally satisfied with these laws and have tinkered with them for years. Street prostitution has been a thorn in the side of the police since the Supreme Court decision on soliciting in 1978. They've consistently pressured the feds for more effective ammunition for use in their war against whores. In the fall of 1985 Parliament introduced Bill c-49 which was intended to toughen up the soliciting law by making it an offence to communicate in public for the purpose of prostitution. This bill led to the creation of Section 213 of the Criminal Code, the well-known communicating law.

At the time Justice Minister John Crosbie vowed the "national disgrace" of street prostitution would end in a week once this new law was approved. In 1983 there were 105 prostitution-related arrests made in Toronto, in 1984 there were 78 and in 1985 Metro Police made 143 prostitution arrests. In 1986 the communicating law took effect and 2,708 prostitution arrests were made in Toronto, 4,211 were made in 1987 and 4,465 in 1988. In the same year that this record number of arrests were made Toronto Mayor Art Eggleton told Justice Minister Ray Hnatyshyn that the communicating law needed more teeth! While the cops busted hookers left and right the number of pros working Toronto's streets increased, something Eggleton said was "unacceptable to the city." Later in 1989 a federal study showed that despite the high number of arrests, and conviction rates that ranged between seventy-five and ninety per cent, street prostitution in Canada hadn't been reduced by the communicating law — John Crosbie's vaunted law was a complete failure.

In 1992 the Commons Justice Committee called for tougher penalties, including taking drivers' licences away from customers convicted of communicating, but Justice Minister Kim Campbell flatly rejected the recommendations. Also in 1992 the constitutionality of the anti-pimping law was challenged. Kenneth Downey of Alberta and Corrine Reynolds, the woman he lived with, were charged with living on the avails of prostitution. Reynolds owned and operated an escort service and Downey occasionally answered the phones and did the banking. Both were convicted but Downey appealed the case to the Supreme Court, on the grounds that the anti-pimping law violates the right of the accused to be presumed innocent until proven guilty. The lower-court decision was upheld by a vote of four to three but dissenting Justice Beverley McLachlin said the law was too broad: "Spouses, lovers, friends, children, parents, room-mates and business associates live with prostitutes and not all of them are pimps."

Interest in prostitution issues continues to rise and fall. Edmonton's city council looked into licensing escort agencies and the idea found favour as far east as Toronto but went nowhere. Edmonton's council forgot that if they licensed the services they would be condoning an activity the courts consider illegal. Prostitution is also a federal issue and you can't just ignore jurisdictional boundaries. In 1994 Liberal Justice Minister Allan Rock said in his maiden speech that the new government will get tough with pimps and other offenders "who make our homes and streets unsafe." A year later Rock promised to crack down on street prostitution — again — by impounding customers' cars, fingerprinting hookers and their clients (both ideas previously rejected by Conservative Justice Minister Kim Campbell) and imposing a mandatory five-year jail term for pimps. Rock's promises came in the wake of a call for the decriminalization of prostitution made by none other than Toronto's city council.

The prostitution laws as they stand now create a ridiculous legal situation for those working in the Business. It's okay to be a prostitute but you can't advertise or talk about your services on the street; you can't work out of your own home or set up a place specifically for work; you can't have friends, lovers or associates; you can't support someone else with your earnings; you can't refer customers to other prostitutes and no one can refer customers to you. Call-girls must always go to their customers rather than have customers come to them. Our politicians must consider prostitutes a particularly horrid group of people because no other group of adults, criminal or otherwise, has so many laws surrounding them which affect their day-to-day lives. If your husband was Pablo Escobar you wouldn't have had to worry about being charged with living on the avails of trafficking in cocaine. Karla Homolka's friends weren't punished for associating with her, but if she had been a whore instead of a killer, technically they could have been charged with pimping.

I cannot remember exactly when I turned my last trick. It was sometime in early 1992, an outcall I think to a downtown Toronto hotel. I can't recall the customer's name, I can't remember what he looked like. The memories of most of my customers are like that. I've kept the notable ones, but the rest have been shunted into a cerebral backwater where they stay until something happens or someone says something and I respond with, "Oh yes, that reminds me ...," as some old memory gets dusted off, a souvenir from a past life.... Every once in a while I see an old trick on the street or in a store or restaurant. We don't acknowledge each other, there are no subtle nods of heads or sly winks. I wonder if they remember.

I didn't rest when I retired from the Biz, I started to write. I had been writing for years; there was the soft porn for Steve; later I wrote on prostitution for CORP's newsletter *Stiletto* and other low-to-the-ground publications. I kept a diary and had two outlines for novels sitting in a file. When Maggie's broke away from CORP in 1992, I faxed every media outlet in Toronto, telling them briefly what had happened and informing them of the new phone numbers and contact people. One of my faxes reached Stevie Cameron, who was writing a weekly column for *The Globe and Mail*. She was intrigued by the political infighting going on among a handful of whores and wannabe social workers and she asked me if I would consent to an interview. I was a regular reader of Stevie's column and had great respect for her as a journalist so I happily agreed. During the spring of 1992 we met and talked many times about prostitution, AIDS, drugs, transition — all the things I'm used to discussing with journalists, but Stevie went further. She asked me if I had anything she could read. I anxiously gave her copies of some of the work I had done over the last three years, expecting a non-committal kind of response.

"Alex, you should be writing for a living," was the first thing she said to me the next time we got together. Not long after that, I sold my first piece to *The Globe and Mail* and Stevie and I collaborated on a feature for *The Financial Post Magazine.* I stopped renewing my escort ads in the entertainment weeklies, changed the message on my answering machine and turned the trick room into a store room. My twenty-year career as a whore was over. I had found something better.

I got out of prostitution at the right time. I suppose I could have stayed in for at least a few more years; the oldest whore I ever met was the seventy-something Elizabeth Spedding, the Contessa. She ran an escort service in Toronto until she passed away in the mid-1990s and rumour has it she turned occasional tricks right up to the end. But I had had my fill of commercial sex and had no desire to stay in prostitution for the next thirty years. Overall the Business treated me well, although I wish there was some sort of a pension package — a golden handshake at least — for retiring hookers. All I managed to take away from the Biz were my experiences and a closet full of work clothes — hooker drag and high-heeled shoes — that I don't wear any more. The good things I have in my life now have not come from prostitution.

When I combine the current realities of earning less money and having to deal with more hassles, I don't think I would get involved in prostitution today if I were nineteen and starting all over. But when I look at the kinds of opportunities available in the workplace today for young people as well as the high cost of living, I can understand why so many feel compelled to start turning tricks.

I used to have an optimistic attitude about the future of prostitution but that has changed. Pros were treated better by their clients in the seventies than in the nineties. Working women had less of a stigma then than now. Prostitutes are still considered by many people to be the vectors of HIV/AIDS even though the Ontario AIDS Network, the Canadian AIDS Society and Health Canada have all publicly stated that pros are not a risk factor when it comes to the transmission of the virus but are at risk of catching the disease from tainted needles (if they're injecting drugs) and infected clients who refuse to use condoms.

The arguments in favour of the decriminalization of voluntary, adult prostitution are so strong, while the continued criminalization of the Business has proven to be so ineffective, that while I was involved in prostitution politics I predicted the laws in Canada would change by the year 2000. Logic dictated this change; no one is happy with our current laws and none of them have enabled the police and the courts to meet their objectives. The number of prostitutes has not gone down, neighbourhoods haven't been protected and prostitution has not been driven underground. As prostitution continues to be visible on our streets, the government will crack down harder on the women and men who are only trying to earn a living. History shows us that this response doesn't work but history also shows us that this is the only response our elected federal officials are comfortable with. The House of Commons has no room for imaginative thinkers and the politicians will inevitably repeat the dismal performances of their predecessors. No one will win.

If I had a daughter I would not want her to become a prostitute. Ordinary citizens blame whores for a wide range of social problems, they're misrepresented by the media and punished by our legal system. I would rather my daughter, or son for that matter, take up a different line of work and I would like to think that my children would have the chance to do so but there are fewer opportunities out there, particularly for women. In spite of the corporate spin, entire categories of jobs have been wiped out by changes in attitudes and advances in technology. Employers and the employed are closing ranks as job security is threatened. I would not want to see my children toiling away at meaningless McJobs which offer no hope for advancement and which don't even pay subsistence wages. If a child of mine chose to prostitute herself, I would make my feelings on the trade known to her and do what I could to ensure her safety. If a daughter or son asked me what I did when I was young, I would explain everything in detail, without hesitation. I would tell my children that as a whore I sold good sex and as an activist for prostitutes' rights I fought the good fight. Nothing else matters.

acknowledgments

The following publications were useful in the writing of this book:

Alexander, Priscilla. *Prostitutes Prevent aids: A Manual for Health Educators.* San Francisco: California Prostitutes Education Project, 1988.

Delacoste, Frédérique and Priscilla Alexander, eds. *Sex Work: Writings by Women in the Sex Industry.* London: Virago Press, 1988.

Bell, Laurie, ed. *Good Girls/Bad Girls: Sex Trade Workers and Feminists Face to Face.* Toronto: The Women's Press, 1987.

Bullough, Vern and Bonnie Bullough. *Women and Prostitution: A Social History.* Buffalo: Prometheus Books, 1987.

Newton, Michael. *Hunting Humans: The Encyclopedia of Serial Killers, Volume II.* New York: Avon Books, 1993.

Barrows, Sydney Biddle and William Novak. *Mayflower Madam: The Secret Life of Sydney Biddle Barrows.* New York: Ballantine Books, 1986.

Roberts, Nickie. *Whores in History: Prostitution in Western Society.* London: Grafton, 1993.

Rodrigues, Gary P., ed. *The 1993 Pocket Criminal Code.* Scarborough, Ontario: Carswell Thomson Professional Publishing, 1993.

Rumbelow, Donald. *Jack the Ripper: The Complete Casebook.* New York: Berkley Books, 1990.

I'm grateful to Michael Sobota, the Executive Director of the AIDS Committee of Thunder Bay, and a truly gentle man, for not holding Karen back, and for giving me an opportunity to try out my voice. I thank Bill Reynolds, editor of *eye Weekly*, and author Stevie Cameron for guiding me through the hustle of journalism; I also thank Stevie for telling me I could — and should — write this book. I thank my agent, Jan Whitford, for doing a great job of introducing my idea to the publishing world; my editor Diane Martin, whose gentle guidance taught me what's hot writing and what's not; and Susan Roxborough, the photographer who caught the essence of my relationship with the little bird Paddy O'Conure.

I also thank the Canada Council's Explorations Program for their generous financial support of this project.